Penguin Handbooks
Easy Cooking for One or Two

Louise Davies left King's College of Household and Social
Science (now Queen Elizabeth College, London
University) with a B.Sc. degree and a conviction that
scientists need interpreting. She has therefore combined
the study of nutrition with writing, broadcasting,
interviewing, lecturing and television appearances.
At the Ministry of Food she wrote a monthly
magazine, *Food and Nutrition*, for dietitians and
domestic science teachers and managed to involve
the whole school curriculum with the subjects.
Her first book, *See How to Cook*, was a pioneer amongst
picture cookery books. For twelve years she broadcast
Shopping List twice weekly in the B.B.C. *Today* programme,
giving advice on shopping and recipe hints, and
combining this and other broadcasts with a busy home
life. Now, as head of the Geriatric Nutrition Unit at
Queen Elizabeth College, she is conducting research into
the nutritional needs of the elderly and is actively
encouraging practical help for those who shop for one
or two. Louise Davies is her maiden name. She was
recently widowed and has two schoolgirl daughters.

Easy Cooking for One or Two

Louise Davies

ILLUSTRATED BY
Tony Odell

Penguin Books

Penguin Books Ltd, Harmondsworth,
Middlesex, England
Penguin Books Australia Ltd, Ringwood,
Victoria, Australia

First published 1972
Reprinted 1972 (three times), 1973

Copyright © Louise Davies, 1972

Made and printed in Great Britain by
Richard Clay (The Chaucer Press) Ltd,
Bungay, Suffolk
Set in Monotype Baskerville

Contents

Foreword   vii

Preface   ix

Acknowledgements   xiii

The Geriatric Nutrition Unit xv

Nutrition on Your Own   1

Recipes for Non-cooks   10

Simple Recipes for One or Two   40

Favourites from the Cookery
   Classes   118

Store-cupboard Cookery   164

Some Useful Hints and
   Information   186

List of Illustrations   203

Index   205

Foreword

Food is a major interest for some, a distraction for others, but for all a necessity. We need it to be well chosen and properly prepared and for many of us those two require-ments are left to others for most of our lives. But many people late in life are suddenly faced with the need to prepare food for themselves, or lose the opportunity and the interest of doing it for more than themselves. Old people left alone, for example recently bereaved widowers, are often ill-prepared to look after themselves and may let their diet become monotonous and often ill-balanced. This book, alone or in conjunction with cookery classes, makes it much easier to plan nourishing meals. In short it is not simply a cook book but in its own way a piece of preventive medicine, and I hope many will find it the help they need.

Sir George Godber,
Chief Medical Officer,
Department of Health
and Social Security

Preface

It is fashionable to talk about an ageing population, to give statistics of the increasing proportion of people that now survive to become elderly or – to use one of the many euphemisms for old age – survive to become senior citizens. We talk, too, of social problems that arise, and especially we talk of their nutritional needs. Do they need the same amounts of calories and protein, of vitamins and minerals, as they did when they were younger, or do they need more, or perhaps less? What sorts of food should they be eating to get these nutrients? What are they in fact eating, and how far are they getting their requirements? And are there alternative foods that would suit them better, because they prefer them, or because they can prepare them more easily, or because they keep better?

Many of these questions continue to require rigid scientific study, for we still do not know all of the answers. It was to try to get some of these answers that in 1968 we set up in this Department the Geriatric Nutrition Unit under the leadership of Miss Louise Davies. She and her colleagues have been finding out whether it is true that people's taste sensitivity and preferences change as they grow older, how they react to particular prepared foods that are already on the market, the extent to which the Meals on Wheels service satisfies their wants as well as their nutritional needs.

But Louise Davies is not content to look at these problems only as part of scientific research. She has taken a great interest in participating in, and initiating, cookery classes for the elderly. She has gained a great deal of experience in knowing what foods the elderly like, what sorts of dishes they can readily prepare, and more particularly how to combine both what they like and what they can make with the essential feature of high nutritional value at reasonable cost.

The recipes in this book show how well Miss Davies has succeeded in producing this combination of features. But she has done much more. The recipes include dishes that are simple to make for the man – or woman – who has had little experience in cooking, but they also include more ambitious dishes that will appeal to the experienced or venturesome. They contain several suggestions for novel dishes, or novel ways of preparing old favourites, so as to help overcome the tendency of lonely, elderly people gradually to lose interest in food because they are eating a monotonous and often badly balanced diet. The recipes have also, every one of them, been tested not only for practicality, but for acceptability by the sorts of people for whom they are designed. They are by no means just the same sort of recipes as those you will find in standard cook books simply scaled down to make a meal for one or two.

I am certain that this book will go a long way towards helping to overcome some of the more difficult problems that face elderly people.

John Yudkin,
Emeritus Professor,
Queen Elizabeth College

Acknowledgements

My thanks to Jeanette Grant for her enthusiastic and invaluable help with the pre-testing of these recipes.

Katie Hastrop, Pamela Cross and Nancy Sienkiewicz also gave practical advice.

Professor John Yudkin has given active encouragement to the work of the Geriatric Nutrition Unit and has helped me by discussing the nutritional details in this book.

I am indebted to all the teachers of Retirement Cookery Classes who sent me recipes and to the students and teachers of the following classes who tested and commented on the recipes:

Almondbury Further Education Centre
Arbroath, Angus
Basford Hall College of Further Education, Nottingham
Braunstone Adult Education Centre, Leicester
Camden Institute, London
Charles Keene College of Further Education, Leicester
Coventry Technical College
The Elms Technical College, Stoke-on-Trent
Harlow Technical College
North Riding of Yorkshire Rural Economics Service

Richmond Adult College, Class for the Blind and Partially
    Sighted, Surrey
Sheffield Polytechnic
Swinton and Pendlebury Adult Education Centre
Wolverhampton College of Adult Education
Wythenshawe Adult Education Centre, Manchester

I thank the following firms for suggesting some of the recipes
in this book. In addition, they will send you free recipe leaflets
suitable for Cooking for One or Two. Mention this book when
writing.

The Atora Kitchen, Ranks Hovis McDougall Foods Ltd,
    10 Victoria Rd, NW10 6 NU
Birds Eye Foods Ltd, Walton on Thames, Surrey
Bovril Ltd, Sunleigh Road, Alperton, Wembley, Middlesex
British Farm Produce Council, Agriculture House, Knights-
    bridge, SW1
Brown & Polson Ltd, 10 New Fetter Lane, EC4
Butter Information Council, Salisbury House, London Wall,
    EC2
Cadbury Schweppes Foods Ltd, Food Advisory Services,
    Bournville, Birmingham
Canned & Packaged Foods Bureau, 37 Baker Street, W1
Delrosa, The Phillips Scott & Turner Co., 2 St Mark's Hill,
    Surbiton, Surrey
Flour Advisory Bureau, 21 Arlington Street, SW1
Food Information Centre, 12 Park Lane, Croydon, Surrey
Milk Marketing Board, Thames Ditton, Surrey
National Dairy Council, 5–7 John Princes Street, W1
Rice Council, 87 Notting Hill Gate, London, W11
Stork Cookery Service, Kildare House, Dorset Rise, EC4

The Geriatric Nutrition Unit

Although we hope the recipes in this book will appeal to 'the bed-sitter brigade' or anyone else who is catering for one or two, they were written primarily for the over sixties.

The dishes have been prepared and eaten by students at 'Over 60s' and 'Retirement' cookery classes throughout the country. They were given a questionnaire asking the following:

> Did they find the recipe easy to make?
> Did they enjoy it?
> Would they make it again at home?

If the answer to all three questions was 'yes', the recipe appears in this book.

The cookery classes helped us even more. On the same questionnaire the students gave their own suggestions and comments. The teachers sent us recipes which had proved to be popular in the classes. These class recipes have been given a special chapter of their own: 'Favourites from the Cookery Classes'.

Throughout this book we have kept to the policy of the Geriatric Nutrition Unit, Queen Elizabeth College, London University: we do not think we should preach to older people and tell them what they should eat. Rather, we are making a good, nourishing diet out of what they *like* to eat.

The Geriatric Nutrition Unit was set up in 1968 to carry out specialized research into problems of nutrition which may affect the health, independence and happiness of the over sixties. It is so far the only unit of its kind in the world but other countries are showing interest in our findings.

Our work is made possible by generous donations from the following sponsors, to whom this book is dedicated:

Bovril Ltd
Cadbury-Schweppes Foods Ltd
The Electrical Association for Women
Flour Advisory Bureau
The Gas Council
H. J. Heinz & Co. Ltd
Marks & Spencer Ltd
Metal Box Company
Milk Marketing Board
Peel Medical Research Fund
Spillers Ltd
Unilever Ltd
United Biscuits Ltd

Chapter 1
Nutrition on Your Own

When you live on your own

- food works out to be more expensive than for larger family catering.
- quantities for one are difficult to find; often you are obliged to buy too much, so left-over food has to be thrown out.
- loneliness may make you lose your appetite; or over-eat the easy, fattening fillers.
- you may not be bothered just to cook for yourself.

For all these reasons and more, your diet – and your health – may suffer.

For those living on their own there are three rules for better eating:

1. EAT A LITTLE OF EVERYTHING AND NOT TOO MUCH OF ANY ONE THING

Do not cut out any food from your normal shopping list unless warned to do so by the doctor. The nourishment your body needs is spread through many different foods. The more variety you eat the better.

2. THERE IS NO FOOD THAT YOU MUST HAVE

Do not listen to the know-alls who insist that you must eat 'raw carrots', or 'liver once a week'. Certainly they are good for you. But millions live for more than three-score years and ten without them. If you positively dislike a certain food, there are always equally nourishing alternatives.

3. MOST FOODS ARE GOOD FOR YOU BUT SOME FOODS ARE NOT QUITE AS GOOD FOR YOU AS OTHERS

The foods which are not quite so good for you are the sugary and starchy foods such as sugar, sweets, biscuits, buns and cakes. Eating these may be the cheapest and easiest way to fill up but too much can lead to obesity. You cannot be healthy if you are obese; if you fall you fall more heavily, if you have illness such as arthritis, heart trouble or bronchitis extra weight makes it worse.

If you want to know more about nutrition, read on. If theory bores you, just remember the three rules above, skip the rest of this chapter and turn to the recipes. They have all been chosen to be especially nourishing, but our panel of testers has made sure that first and foremost they are easy to buy and prepare, and good to eat.

FOODS FOR BODY BUILDING

Some people feel that once they are fully grown there is very little body building left to be done. But there they are wrong. All parts of the body are continuously breaking down and having to be replaced by body-building foods. The main foods for body building are MEAT and POULTRY, FISH, MILK, CHEESE and EGGS; also some vegetable foods especially PEAS and BEANS and LENTILS.

Traditional dishes (not through knowledge of nutrition, but just by happy chance) often combined a wise nourishing mixture of animal and vegetable, e.g. FISH and CHIPS, BREAD and CHEESE, PORRIDGE and MILK.

In countries such as Britain, where there is an ample supply of food, it is unusual for anyone to go short of the body-building foods. However there are times when there is a call for extra body-builders, for example:

- after operations and during convalescence.
- where there has been semi-starvation (possibly through incapacity, bereavement or loneliness in old age) and more flesh needs to be put back on wasted bodies.
- when body-builders, particularly meat, have been neglected because of price.
- when body-builders, particularly meat, have been neglected because they are difficult to chew.

To make sure you are eating enough of the body-building foods we have included many recipes using the foods listed above. There is no space to mention them all here, but below are a few examples:

Inexpensive Meat Dishes	*Page*	*Easy-to-chew Meat Dishes*	*Page*
Sweet and Sour Spare-ribs	161	Meat Balls	82
Meat Stew Norwegian Style	84	Cottage Pie	66
Lancashire Hot-pot	76	Ham and Vegetable Rice	172
Steak Pan Pudding	106	Bacon Pudding	46
Bacon or Ham with Mustard Sauce	44	Spaghetti Bolognese	180
Meat Roly-poly	173	Pilaff	91

Quick and Easy Dishes	*Page*	*Tempting for Convalescents*	*Page*
Cheese 'Pizza'	14	Egg Flip	17
Golden Cutlet and Egg Sauce	138	Lazy Soup	23
Goulash	171	Yogurt Jelly	38
Soup Scramble	179	Baked Custard	166
Toasted Cheese	37	Quick Fish Soufflé	98
Poached Eggs	31	Steamed Roasting Chicken with Egg and Lemon Sauce	108

Other Inexpensive
Body-builders   *Page*   *Page*

Lentil Cream Soup   141   Cheese and Ketchup
Potato and Cheese   Toasted Sandwich   13
   Savoury Custard   152   Herring Roes on
Grilled Cod   75   Toast   173
                                   Savoury Milk -   32

FOODS FOR HEALTHY BLOOD

Nutritional anaemia is one of the lowering illnesses which is found particularly in some young women and in the elderly. The nutrient lacking in the blood is iron.

The main foods which provide IRON are:

MEATS, especially LIVER, HEART, KIDNEY and CORNED BEEF; EGGS, GREEN VEGETABLES.

If your doctor tells you that you are anaemic try to cook some of the many dishes in this book which include these ingredients. Here are a few examples:

Suggested Recipes
for Iron   *Page*   *Page*

Liver-sausage and   Corned Beefburgers   17
   Egg Spread   34   Liver and Bacon
Devilled Kidneys   68   Bake   80

COCOA, CURRY POWDER, BLACK TREACLE and DRIED FRUIT are examples of other iron-containing foods, but they are only eaten in small quantities, so do not rely on these foods. Nevertheless, even small quantities will help to provide some of your requirements.

VITAMIN C FOODS

Vitamin C is needed for healthy gums and to speed the healing of cuts and ulcers and for general vitality.

Vitamin C is found to an appreciable extent in FRUITS and VEGETABLES especially in the CITRUS fruits (ORANGES, GRAPEFRUIT and LEMONS), BLACK-CURRANTS, STRAWBERRIES, CABBAGE, BRUSSELS SPROUTS, CAULIFLOWER and POTATOES. There are also the VITAMIN C DRINKS such as orange juice, blackcurrant juice and rose-hip syrup (but make sure that vitamin C is mentioned on the label). Note that FROZEN fruit and vegetables are an excellent source of vitamin C and so are many CANNED varieties. Drying is more destructive of the vitamin but some manufacturers, knowing this, add vitamin C to the dried food.

You may miss some vitamin C from your diet because

- many of the foods mentioned above are expensive.
- the citrus fruits may be troublesome to peel, or they may sting sore gums or lips.
- most of the vitamin C in vegetables may be lost by poor cooking methods or long storage.
- you may find raw salad vegetables indigestible.

Vitamin C cannot be stored in the body so fresh supplies should be taken quite frequently – at least 2–3 times a week, preferably every day.

To be sure of good supplies turn to recipes such as:

Suggested Recipes for Vitamin C	*Page*		*Page*
Green Vegetables, How to Cook	19	Apple with Amber Sauce	41
Lemonade	25	Blackcurrant Pudding	51
		Peptail	29

BONE BUILDING FOODS

One of the scourges of advancing age is the ease with which bones fracture. A good supply of calcium which helps to make strong bones and teeth is found in MILK, CHEESE and BREAD.

To help to put the calcium into the bones and teeth, vitamin D must also be available. The main foods which provide vitamin D are:

FAT FISH, BUTTER, MARGARINE and CHEESE (except cheeses made from skim milk). Vitamin D also comes through SUNSHINE.

Older people sometimes miss valuable vitamin D because

- they may wear cover-up clothing and tend to avoid hot sunlight; sunlight makes vitamin D in the skin.
- fat fish, such as herrings and kippers, contain many small off-putting bones.

However in canned fatty fish, bones are soft enough to eat to give you both calcium and vitamin D, so try to eat SARDINES, PILCHARDS, TUNA and CANNED SALMON.

Among the recipes for bone building are:

Suggested Recipes for Bone Building

	Page		Page
Digestible Sardine	34	Cheese Soufflé, One-stage	61
Tuna and Tomato Spread	35	Cheese and Marmite Bread and Butter Pudding	58
Potato and Milk Soup	153		

FOODS FOR ENERGY

All foods so far mentioned provide energy, needed for every body movement as well as for warmth. The sugars, starches and fats are the first to be used for energy and warmth. When people are starved of these, the foods which should be used for body building may have to be used for energy instead.

You can take it for granted that if you are not hungry and are not losing weight, you are eating enough to satisfy your energy requirements, so you need not search for recipes using sugar, starches and fats. In fact, if you need to slim, cut down on these foods.

In order to release the energy for use by the body, vitamins of the B group are also needed. These are widespread in foods and easily obtainable if you have a varied diet. For instance, they can be found in MEAT, including LIVER and KIDNEY; FLOUR, BREAD, YEAST and YEAST EXTRACT (e.g. Marmite), BACON, COD'S ROE, MILK and MILK PRODUCTS.

I hope that the recipes containing these recommended foods – and all the other recipes in this book – will tempt you to enjoy eating.

Chapter 2
Recipes for Non-cooks

This chapter is for the times when you do not feel like cooking. It is also for those of you who have never had to cook and are now having to manage on your own. The recipes need scarcely any effort but they are nourishing as well as tempting.

There are a number of more adventurous recipes in the other chapters. You should find them easy to cook. Here are some examples and you may like to look for others:

	Page		Page
California Salad	125	Fruit Muesli	137
Chocolate Mousse	169	Soup Scramble	179
Bacon or Ham with		Spaghetti Bolognese	180
Mustard Sauce	44	Spiced Grapefruit	104
Golden Cutlet and		Summer Fish	112
Bacon	74	Summer Cup	184
Grilled Herring No. 2	139	Welsh Rarebit	116

Hot meals are satisfying and enjoyable and most people aim to have at least one cooked meal a day. However it is quite possible to be well nourished without this.

It is not true that you can keep warm in winter only by eating hot food. Certainly, hot food is more inviting in cold weather but your body can keep warm from any nourishing food, hot or cold. If you feel you cannot face the chore of cooking, you may be tempted by ready-prepared nourishing cold snacks. Look for the sliced meats, ready-prepared salads, pickled herrings, smoked cod's roe, cheeses, scotch eggs, meat pies, yogurts, milk desserts and similar foods. It is better to have these and relax than to force yourself to cook when you do not feel like it.

'Afternoon Nap' Tea

This is invaluable for those who are bed-ridden – the tray can be prepared for them in advance. For those who just feel tired, put this at the ready before you take a nap. It is then not necessary to go and put the kettle on when you wake up, just pop the tea-bag into the flask.
You need a half-pint vacuum flask.

Serves 1

1   Take a tray with a half-pint vacuum flask almost filled with boiling water.
2   Also put on the tray one tea-bag, milk and sugar, if liked, cup, saucer and spoon.

3   When required, drop the tea-bag in the flask, and
     allow 3–5 minutes infusion, with cap replaced.
     (You may be surprised to find that it does not matter

     that the water is not 'on the boil' when the tea is
     made, but this vacuum-flask method is only suitable
     for tea-bags otherwise you will get floating tea-
     leaves.)
4   Pour yourself a cup of tea to your liking.

Cheese and Ketchup Toasted Sandwich
or
Cheese and Ham Toasted Sandwich

An ordinary cheese sandwich is a nourishing snack. But a hot toasted sandwich makes a more satisfying, tempting meal.

Serves 1

Cooking time: approximately 8 minutes

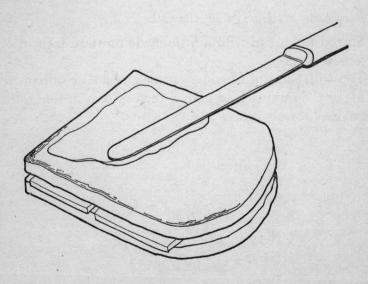

INGREDIENTS

a little butter – kept in the   tomato ketchup, or your
  warm to soften it   favourite chutney or pickle
2 slices of bread   Cheddar cheese, sliced

METHOD

1 Spread the bread with tomato ketchup.
2 Place cheese in the middle to make an unbuttered
   sandwich at this stage.
3 Now spread the outsides of the sandwich with butter.
4 Place on grill-grid and grill each side till golden
   brown, using your knife and fork for turning. Serve
   piping hot.

For Cheese and Ham as an Alternative Filling

Spread the bread with a little made mustard instead of
tomato ketchup.
Top with slices of Cheddar cheese and a slice of ham.
Make the sandwich as above, then grill each side until
golden brown.

Cheese 'Pizza'

1–2 servings

Cooking time: approximately 10 minutes

INGREDIENTS

2 rashers streaky bacon
(rinds removed, rashers
cut into 3)
1 bap or soft bread roll (cut
in half)

2 oz. Cheddar cheese
(sliced and crumbled)
1 tomato (sliced)

METHOD

1 Place bacon on top of bap and grill gently until bacon
is cooked and bap lightly browned – about 5–6
minutes.
2 Place cheese and tomato on top of bacon and grill
lightly until cheese just begins to melt.

CODDLED EGGS – FOOLPROOF METHOD

How many times have you heard 'she can't even boil an
egg'? But boiling an egg is not a job any fool can do,
unless one is clever enough to use the foolproof method.
Our method is more correctly called 'coddling' because
the egg, though tasting like a boiled egg, is not actually
boiled for more than a few seconds, but is merely left in
very hot water.

Coddled Eggs (soft)

1   If the eggs are kept in a refrigerator it is best to allow them to regain room temperature by taking them out of the fridge 2 to 3 hours, at least, before using.
2   In a small pan bring water to the boil. It must be a fast rolling boil. The quantity must be enough to cover the eggs when they are put in.
3   Using a spoon, lower the eggs into the water.
4   Turn out the heat, immediately cover the pan and remove from the heat.
5   Allow to stand for 8 minutes.

Coddled Eggs (hard)

1   Remove eggs from refrigerator as before.
2   Place the eggs in a pan of cold water, covering them with at least a quarter of an inch of water.
3   Bring to the boil over medium–fast heat.
4   Turn out the heat, immediately cover the pan and remove from the heat.
5   Allow to stand for 15 minutes.
6   Take out the eggs and immediately plunge them into cold (preferably running) water to stop them cooking further and producing the unappetizing black ring which appears between white and yolk when eggs are overcooked.

Corned Beefburgers

Serves 2

INGREDIENTS

a 7-oz. can of corned beef
seasoned flour (flour mixed
   with a little salt and
   pepper)

margarine, dripping or fat
   for frying
vegetables and fried eggs for
   a more substantial meal, if
   liked

METHOD

1   Cut the corned beef into slices half an inch thick.
2   Dip in seasoned flour.
3   Fry, then drain, using absorbent paper if you have it.
4   Serve with vegetables or, for a supper dish, add a
     fried egg.

Egg Flip

Serves 1

INGREDIENTS

1 egg
1 level teaspoon sugar (or to
   taste)

2 teaspoons sherry or brandy
three quarters of a mug of
   milk

METHOD

1   Beat together the egg, sugar and sherry or brandy
     until smooth.

2   Heat the milk in a saucepan, but do not allow to boil.
3   Stir briskly into the mixture and serve at once in a tumbler or mug.

Egg and Onion

Serves 1

INGREDIENTS

1 small onion
a knob of butter or
   margarine

2 standard eggs
salt and pepper

METHOD

1   Peel and slice onion fairly thinly.
2   Fry in butter or margarine until softened but not browned.
3   Beat the eggs well with a fork or whisk and add seasoning to taste.
4   Pour the eggs on to onions and stir until scrambled.
5   Serve immediately.

This was my mother-in-law's favourite weekend supper snack. With it she served buttered water-biscuits, as a change from toast.

GREEN VEGETABLES – QUICK AND NOURISHING

1   Wash and prepare only just before use.

    (a) Brussels sprouts are best trimmed of outer, discoloured leaves, then cut down in half. This enables you to see whether they are clean right through, and also cuts down the cooking time because half sprouts cook through more quickly than whole sprouts. Wash them well in salted cold water before cooking.

    (b) Cabbage should be shredded with a sharp knife and washed just before cooking. Shredded cabbage cooks more quickly than cabbage merely cut in halves or quarters.

    (c) Cauliflower should be cleaned carefully in salted water, particular attention being paid to the base of the stems where dirt collects. Cut a cross in the bottom stem, after trimming it, to allow the heat to penetrate through the stem more quickly.

    (d) Greens can be torn into rough pieces just before cooking.

2   Cook in the *minimum* of fast-boiling, lightly salted water, with the lid tightly on the pan so that the vegetables are mostly cooking in steam.

    If you use too much water (an inch in the pan is generally sufficient) or leave the lid off, valuable vitamin C can escape.

    Cauliflowers need more water (a pan half filled with boiling water once the vegetable is in). To keep the flower white, place the flower-side down for the first five minutes then turn stem-side down till cooked (about 20 minutes in all).

The other vegetables listed are generally just-cooked in 5 minutes.

3 Serve immediately. Keeping vegetables warm also destroys vitamin C.

Health Food Cereal

This is a useful standby: an 'eat-when-you-fancy' dish.

Serves 1

INGREDIENTS

1 eating apple
1 teaspoon wheat germ
  (Bemax or Froment)
1 teaspoon rose-hip syrup
a few sultanas or seedless
  raisins

3 tablespoons, or more, top of
  the milk
a portion of cornflakes or
  your favourite cereal

METHOD

1 Grate the apple coarsely into a cereal bowl. (There is no need to peel the apple unless you wish.)

2 Stir in wheat germ, rose-hip syrup, sultanas and top of the milk.

3 Just before serving, add the cereal, plus extra milk if you like.

Kippers

To avoid cooking smells, one of the best ways to cook kippers is to place the kipper or kipper fillets in a jug or shallow dish and pour boiling water over them. Cover the jug or dish with a lid, a plate or with foil. Leave without further heating for 5 minutes. Drain off the water and you will find the kippers cooked to perfection.

Note: sometimes a large kipper or a packet of kipper fillets is too much for one meal. Any left-overs can be flaked, kept cool and covered, and used the next day for kipper scramble.

Kipper Scramble

Serves 1

INGREDIENTS

1 kipper fillet
2 standard eggs
pepper

a knob of butter or margarine
a slice of buttered toast

METHOD

1   After cooking the kipper by the above method remove the skin and flake the fish whilst it is warm.
2   Beat the eggs, season with pepper but not salt, and add flaked kipper.

3 Melt knob of butter in a saucepan, pour in the egg mixture. Keep the heat low.

4 Stir the mixture continuously until the eggs are creamy and soft. Remove from the heat just before the mixture looks fully set as cooking continues in the heat of the pan.

5 Serve at once on buttered toast.

Alternative

Scrambled Haddock and Eggs

If you have some smoked haddock left over after a meal, flake the leftover fish free from bones and keep – *cool and covered* – till next day.

If you are starting with a piece of raw, smoked haddock, put it in a pan, just cover it with water, bring to the boil and simmer very gently for a minute or two. Then flake it free from bones.

Serves 1

INGREDIENTS

a knob of butter or margarine
a little flaked, cooked,
   smoked haddock

2 tablespoons milk
2 standard eggs

METHOD

1   Melt the margarine or butter in a small pan. Put the flaked, smoked fish with the milk into the pan and bring to the boil.
2   Break in two standard eggs and stir vigorously with a fork until just before the mixture looks fully set, as cooking continues in the heat of the pan.
3   Serve with hot buttered toast.

Lazy Soup

Comment from Arbroath, Angus: 'We thought it easy and nourishing and a nice change.'

Serves 1

Cooking time: only a few minutes

INGREDIENTS

1 scant cup of water
1 teaspoon Marmite
or 1 teaspoon Bovril

or half a chicken bouillon
  cube
1 standard egg

METHOD

1   In a small pan, bring the water to the boil.
2   Stir in the Marmite, or Bovril, or the bouillon cube and dissolve it. Leave over low heat.
3   Beat the egg well with a fork in a small jug or cup.

4   Lift the jug or cup well above the soup and pour in a
    thin trickle. Do not stir.
    The egg sets in a soft thick 'vermicelli'.
5   Serve immediately before the egg has time to set hard.

Lemonade

This makes a whole pint of lemonade from just one lemon. By keeping it in a covered glass jug you help to preserve the vitamin C overnight. You may have heard – correctly – that vitamin C is destroyed by storage. This is especially true of vegetables. But the acid of the lemon juice helps to preserve it from one day to the next.

INGREDIENTS

1 lemon   half a pint of cold water
one and a half rounded
   tablespoons castor sugar

METHOD

1 Wash the lemon and peel thinly just the outer yellow part of the rind.
2 Put it in a glass jug.
3 Squeeze the lemon and add the juice to the rind in the jug.
4 Stir in the sugar and water.
5 Leave it overnight, covered, in a cold, dark larder or – better still – in the refrigerator.
6 Next day, stir it again and make up to about a pint with cold water but taste it as you go along because you want it to have a tangy refreshing flavour.

Mock Zabaglione

Serves 1

INGREDIENTS

1 egg
1 tablespoon Nestlé
  condensed milk

1 tablespoon sweet sherry or
  Marsala

METHOD

1   Separate the yolk from the white of the egg and mix
    with the condensed milk and sherry or Marsala.
2   Whip up the white of the egg until it is stiff and fold
    it carefully into the mixture using a metal spoon.
3   Serve at once in a glass, with a sponge finger-biscuit.

Mumbled Eggs

Serves 1

Cooking time: 2 or 3 minutes

This is an old-fashioned British recipe, popular in the
days when our ancestors had longer, larger and more
relaxed breakfasts than we do today. Mumbled eggs
could have been just one of a whole series of dishes from
which the well-to-do family helped themselves.

I am told that 'mumbled' means they are easy to eat,
even if you have no teeth. This recipe is ideal for the

beginner in cookery or anyone in a hurry, because there is not much washing up, especially if you use a flame-proof oven-to-table pan.

INGREDIENTS

a knob of butter or margarine   salt and pepper
2 standard eggs

METHOD

1   Melt the butter or margarine in a pan.
2   Just break the fresh eggs into the fat without bother-ing to beat them first.
3   Add a generous pinch of salt and a sprinkle of pepper.
4   Stir vigorously with a fork till just set lightly. Remove from the heat when they are still slightly too liquid to eat: the warmth of the pan will finish cooking them.
5   Serve at once with toast, bread and butter, water-biscuit or crispbread.

Nourishing Breakfast

Serves 1

INGREDIENTS

1 egg
half a cup of cold milk
1 teaspoon to 1 dessertspoon
   rose-hip syrup or vitamin
   C blackcurrant drink

portion of cornflakes,
   Kelloggs 'K' or other
   favourite cereal

METHOD

1 With a fork, beat the egg in a cup.
2 Add the milk (to save using another cup to measure, reckon that the egg plus half a cup of milk almost fills a normal-sized cup).
3 Stir in the rose-hip or blackcurrant (amount according to taste).
4 Strain over the cereal to remove the thread of egg white and serve.

Note. There is no flavour of raw egg in this dish – it just makes a pleasantly rich, creamy milk.

Orange Rice

Serves 1

INGREDIENTS

1 small can creamed rice pudding, or some home-made rice pudding (see page 100)

1 tablespoon frozen orange juice, thawed and undiluted

METHOD

1 Empty the rice into a bowl and stir in the thawed undiluted orange juice.
2 Serve cold or chilled.
   Use the rest of the juice, diluted, for refreshing drinks (try it for Peptail (page 29) for the next day's breakfast).

Alternative

Hot Chocolate Rice

Serves 1

INGREDIENTS

1 small can creamed rice
pudding, or some home-
made rice pudding (see
page 100)

1 tablespoon drinking
chocolate

METHOD

1   Turn out the rice pudding into a small saucepan.
2   Stir in the chocolate powder.
3   Heat gently, stirring.

Note. Try served with sliced raw banana.

Peptail

Try this for breakfast or elevenses – it is a particularly
nourishing beginning to the day if you do not fancy a
cooked breakfast.

Serves 1

INGREDIENTS

1 egg
the juice of 1 large orange
or, a small glass of canned
    orange juice

or, a small glass of diluted
    frozen orange juice

METHOD

1 In a jug, whisk the egg and orange juice together.
2 Strain out the small thread of the egg white by
   pouring through a strainer into a glass.
3 Serve as cold as possible.

Notes. There is no flavour of raw egg in this refreshing
pick-me-up.

The juice of the fresh orange was preferred by the
classes, but the others might make easier alternatives.

Pineapple Salad

Serves 2

Preparation time: a few minutes

INGREDIENTS

2 or 3 lettuce leaves
2 pineapple rings
4 teaspoons cottage cheese

2 teaspoons oil
1 teaspoon vinegar
salt, pepper and sugar

METHOD

1 Arrange lettuce on two plates.
2 Place pineapple rings on top.

3 Fill pineapple centre with cottage cheese.
4 Stir up oil, vinegar and seasonings to make a salad
   dressing, and pour over.

Poached Eggs, Cream-style

Serves 1

Cooking time: about 5 minutes

You need a *small* frying-pan or flameproof oven-to-table
dish

INGREDIENTS

a small knob of butter   1 large or two standard eggs
2 tablespoons or more top of   salt and pepper
   the milk   one slice buttered toast

METHOD

1 Melt the butter in a *small* frying-pan, add top of the
   milk and bring to the boil.
2 Break egg or eggs into a cup and slip them gently
   into the bubbling 'cream'. Season with a little salt
   and pepper.
3 Reduce the heat slightly so that it simmers rather
   than boils and poach the egg for 3 to 5 minutes, or
   to your liking, basting it from time to time with the
   'cream'.
4 Serve on buttered toast.

Savoury Milk

A comforting drink for elevenses or nightcap

The version using the chicken stock cube can be served as a milky chicken soup for lunch.

INGREDIENTS

a cup of hot milk   *or* half a chicken stock cube
1 level teaspoon Bovril or
  Marmite

METHOD

Stir the Bovril, Marmite or chicken stock cube into the very hot milk until it dissolves.

Soup Supper

This simple recipe turns an ordinary bowl of soup into a substantial supper.

Serves 2

INGREDIENTS

1 can ready-to-serve cream of   1 level tablespoon cornflour
  tomato soup   2 level teaspoons Marmite

METHOD

1   Blend the cornflour with 2 tablespoons of cold water.
2   Heat the soup, and when nearly boiling remove from

the heat and stir in the cornflour mixture and the Marmite.
3   Return to heat, stir until boiling and simmer for 3 minutes.
4   Serve hot with toast fingers or toasted cheese (see page 37).

Alternative: if you prefer, serve

Tomato Soup and Egg

Serves 2

INGREDIENTS

1 can ready-to-serve cream of tomato soup

a little milk (optional)
one hard-boiled egg

METHOD

1   Hard boil the egg – or see Coddled Egg (hard) on page 16.
2   Heat the tomato soup, with or without a little added milk.
3   Serve the soup with half a hard-boiled egg in each soup plate. Eat with a spoon, chopping the egg into small pieces.

SAVOURY SPREADS

Digestible Sardine

INGREDIENTS

1 can sardines   1 small egg

METHOD

1   Drain the sardines from the oil, and mash.
2   Beat the egg and gradually add to the mashed sardines to make a smooth mixture. Serve on hot toast.

Notes. Sardines mixed like this with raw beaten egg seem to be more digestible. This pleasant spread could also be served with salad.

Liver-sausage and Egg

INGREDIENTS

1 egg   2 oz. liver-sausage, or small tin of pâté

METHOD

1   Hard boil the egg, cool and chop.
2   Mix with the liver-sausage.

Tuna and Tomato

INGREDIENTS

1 small can tuna fish or pink   3 tablespoons tomato ketchup
  salmon

METHOD

1   Flake the fish with a fork.
2   Blend well with the tomato ketchup.

SWEET SPREADS

Chocolate Spread

INGREDIENTS

2 oz. soft, easy-creaming   1 tablespoon condensed milk
  margarine   vanilla essence, or grated
2 tablespoons cocoa powder   orange rind
half a tablespoon black
  treacle

METHOD

1   Mix the margarine, cocoa powder, treacle and
    condensed milk well together.

2   Add grated orange rind or one or two drops of
    vanilla essence to flavour.
3   Serve on fruit bread, malt bread or buns, or use as a
    cake filling.

Note. This spread keeps for a month in a screw-topped
jar or sealed polythene pot in a cold larder or refrigerator.

Lemon Curd Spread

INGREDIENTS

1 small can condensed milk   rind and juice of a lemon
1 yolk of egg

METHOD

1   Beat all ingredients together.
2   Leave for two hours to thicken before using as a
    spread on bread and butter, or as a cake filling.

Notes. This is an easy method of making lemon curd
with a delicious home-made flavour.
    To use up the egg white, whip it into a fruit jelly on
the point of setting – this makes a light easy dessert.

            *

Tea Grog

Serves 1

INGREDIENTS

boiling water   1 teaspoon sugar, or to taste
tea or 1 tea-bag   1 good slice lemon, or 1
2 teaspoons rum   teaspoon pure lemon juice

METHOD

1   Make the tea in the usual way in a covered teapot,
    allow three minutes infusion. (It is best not to make
    this tea too strong.)
    When you warm the teapot, warm a half-pint
    drinking glass* or mug with hot water at the same
    time and empty just before required.
2   Put all the ingredients into the glass, fill up with tea
    and stir.

   *Use Pyrex 'drink-up' or some similar strong glass in a
holder.

Toasted Cheese

Serves 1

Cooking time: about 5 minutes

INGREDIENTS

a medium-thick slice of bread   Cheddar cheese

METHOD

1 Toast the bread on one side under the grill.
2 Slice the cheese thinly and put, slightly overlapping, over the entire surface of the untoasted side of the bread.
3 Toast the cheese until it melts and begins to bubble and brown. Do not overcook. Serve at once.

Note. A little tomato ketchup can be shaken on the bread under the cheese before toasting.

Yogurt

Yogurt makes an excellent, light, easy to eat and very digestible dessert. It is a dairy product and contains all the goodness of milk. In fact it has a high protein content as extra skimmed-milk powder is added to give the product a firmer consistency. The fat content is, of course, lower in the 'low fat' and 'fat free' products.

As the process involved in its production makes yogurt very digestible, its consumption may possibly aid indigestion, constipation and colitis.

Try mixing the plain yogurt with pieces of fruit (e.g. fresh orange), stewed fruit, blackcurrant vitamin C drink, or fresh lemon juice and sugar to taste. Or you may prefer the sweetened fruit variety.

Yogurt Jelly

Even if you do not fancy yogurt, try this jelly: it tastes like an extra-special milk jelly.

Serves 2–3 – keeps well from one day to the next

INGREDIENTS

half a packet of jelly, your own choice of flavour
boiling water

a 5-oz. carton plain yogurt (or, better still, a flavoured or fruit yogurt to match the flavour of the jelly)

METHOD

1   Place the jelly cubes in a heatproof measuring jug and pour on the boiling water up to the half-pint mark. Stir until dissolved.

2   Leave until cool, but not completely set. Add the yogurt, whisking it in or stirring it briskly with a fork, until it is all blended.

3   Pour into a dish, or separate dishes, and leave to set. This jelly is not quite stiff enough to turn out.

Chapter 3
Simple Recipes for
One or Two

The recipes in this chapter, as in all the other chapters, are arranged in alphabetical order to help you to find them with the greatest ease.

You may often feel like cooking only one dish and having a ready-prepared first course or dessert. For those of you who wish to make fuller use of your oven, I have suggested ten two-course menus (recipes from this chapter and chapter 4: 'Favourites from the Cookery Classes') in which both first and second courses are cooked at the same oven temperature.

Menu No. 1

Baked Brisket
Apple with Amber
    Sauce

Menu No. 2

Bacon or Ham with Mus-
    tard Sauce
Fruit Flapjack

Menu No. 3

Baked Cod
Potato Scones and Syrup

Menu No. 4

Cheese Crumb Chicken
Potatoes Baked in Jackets
Spiced Grapefruit

Menu No. 5

Cheese and Marmite
  Bread and Butter Pudding
Apple Parcel

Menu No. 6

Sweet and Sour Spare-
  ribs of Lamb
Pineapple Meringue
  Pudding

Menu No. 7

Cod Charlotte
Lemon Sponge Pudding

Menu No. 8

Beef Loaf
Rhubarb Bread and
  Butter Pudding

Menu No. 9

Quick Fish Soufflé
Apple (Farmer's Wife)

Menu No. 10

Potato and Cheese
  Savoury Custard
Pineapple Upside-
  down Pudding

Every recipe in the book is clearly marked with oven temperatures and time of cooking so that you can make up more menus of your own.

The chapters also include many top-of-the-stove recipes for both first course and dessert.

Apple with Amber Sauce

Serves 1

Oven temperature: 350°F, gas mark 4

Cooking time: 40 minutes to 1 hour

INGREDIENTS

1 medium cooking apple   1 teaspoon lemon juice*
2 cloves (optional)   1 tablespoon rose-hip syrup
2 tablespoons water

   * If you have a 'sweet tooth', you can add *1 teaspoon clear
honey* to the lemon juice and rose-hip syrup; or drop sultanas,
raisins or chopped dates into the middle of the apple.

METHOD

1   Core whole unpeeled apple.
2   Slit skin with a pointed knife right round centre of
    apple to prevent it bursting. Push a couple of cloves
    into the apple.
3   Place in ovenproof dish. Add the water. (If you like,
    put sultanas, raisins or chopped dates into hole left
    by removal of core.)
4   Bake in moderate oven (350°F, gas mark 4), until
    the apple is soft. This may take anything from 40
    minutes to 1 hour, depending on the variety of apple.
5   Stir together lemon juice, (honey if used) and rose-
    hip syrup.
6   Pour mixture over the apple when removed from the
    oven, and serve.

   Comment from teacher at Harlow Technical College:
'Most of the students had never tasted rose-hip syrup
before. They all liked it but felt it might be rather
expensive for them to buy. However, I pointed out to
them how rich it is in vitamin C and how valuable that

is. All were surprised that no sugar needed to be added to the apple.'

The class at Almondbury Further Education Centre liked the addition of dates, sultanas or raisins for a little extra sweetness.

Apple (Farmer's Wife)

Serves 2

Oven temperature: 375°F, gas mark 5

Cooking time: 30 minutes

INGREDIENTS

1 medium- to large-sized cooking apple

1 level tablespoon brown sugar

1 tablespoon water

Topping

2 oz. Cheddar cheese, grated, or sliced and crumbled

2 oz. seedless raisins

METHOD

1 Peel, core and slice apple, and arrange in a shallow buttered pie dish.
2 Sprinkle the sugar and water over the sliced apple.
3 Cover, use foil if no available lid, and bake in a moderately hot oven (375°F, gas mark 5) for about 25 minutes, or until apple is tender.

4 To make topping: lightly mix cheese and raisins, remove dish from the oven and cover the apple evenly with the mixture.

5 Return to oven uncovered for about 5 minutes, until cheese has just begun to melt. Serve at once.

Bacon or Ham with Mustard Sauce

Serves 2

Note. If you want it to serve one, halve the amount of bacon or ham but keep to the full quantity of sauce.
Oven temperature: 400°F, gas mark 6

Cooking time: 25–30 minutes

INGREDIENTS

2 *thick-cut* lean rashers (long back or collar) or 2 ham steaks

1 tablespoon made mustard (or use 1 tablespoon dry mustard powder plus a little water)

1 level tablespoon soft brown sugar

2 level teaspoons plain flour

4 tablespoons milk

METHOD

1 Remove the rind and place the rashers or the ham steaks in a casserole.

2 Mix the mustard, sugar and flour together and add the milk gradually, stirring well, until smooth. Pour over the rashers, and cover the casserole.

3 Bake in a pre-heated oven (400°F, gas mark 6) for 25–30 minutes.

4 Dish up the rashers on to a hot serving dish or plates, stir the sauce in the casserole and pour over the rashers.

Bacon Joint, Glazed

Serves 4: enough for a hot meal for 2 on one day and a cold meal for 2 on the second day

Oven temperature: 375°F, gas mark 5 for 10 minutes, after preliminary 30 minutes simmer on top of stove

INGREDIENTS

a one-and-a-quarter to one-and-a-half-lb. bacon joint
1 teaspoon black treacle

1 tablespoon brown sugar
2 teaspoons made mustard
2 tablespoons sherry or water

METHOD

1 Place bacon in pan of cold water. Bring to the boil and simmer for 30 minutes. (You may find it necessary to throw off the water once it has boiled, to remove excess salty flavour, and then bring to the boil again with fresh water and simmer. This is not

generally necessary with small ready-to-cook packed joints.)

2   Remove bacon from water. Strip off any rind. Mix treacle, sugar, mustard and sherry or water to a smooth paste and spread over the fat on top of the bacon joint.

3   Place in a small roasting tin in fairly hot oven (375°F, gas mark 5) for 10-15 minutes, *basting frequently* to avoid drying out.

Bacon Pudding

Although this recipe calls for mincing or grating three separate items, we felt it worth including because it is so economical.

Serves 2 or 3 – good served cold next day

Cooking time: 1 hour, 30 minutes to 2 hours

INGREDIENTS

half an oz. of margarine, melted

half a pint (or one large cup) soft breadcrumbs

1 egg, beaten

half a level teaspoon mixed herbs

4 oz. of bacon pieces ⎱ minced
1 small onion   ⎰ together

2 oz. cheese, grated or crumbled

METHOD

1   Mix all ingredients together (note – no seasoning is required because bacon is salty).
2   Pack into a small well-greased 1-pint basin.
3   Cover with kitchen foil or tie on a double thickness of greaseproof paper.
4   Steam, or stand the bowl in a pan of boiling water, topping up the water occasionally so that it stays about two thirds up the outside of the bowl. Steam with the lid tightly on the pan for one and a half to two hours.
5   Serve hot with greens and potatoes and tomato sauce, or cold with salad.

Baked Brisket

Serves 4: two servings hot one day, two servings cold the next

Oven temperature: 400°F, gas mark 6, reduced to 350°F, gas mark 4

Cooking time: 1 hour, 20 minutes

INGREDIENTS

a one-and-a-half-lb. joint of fresh brisket of beef, boned and rolled
salt and pepper
1 lb. of parsnips

three quarters of a pound of potatoes
2 oz. sage and onion stuffing (packet stuffing is easiest)

METHOD

1 Place the seasoned joint in a roasting tin without any
   additional fat, and bake at 400°F, gas mark 6 for
   20 minutes to seal the meat. Reduce temperature
   to 350°F, gas mark 4.
2 Add the parsnips, cut into chunks, and the peeled
   potatoes, cut to the same size as the parsnips. Season
   with salt.
3 Form the stuffing into 6 small cakes and add them to
   the parsnips and potatoes in the tin – by now
   sufficient fat will have come from the beef to baste
   the vegetables.
4 Continue baking at 350°F, gas mark 4 for 1 hour.
5 Drain the vegetables and meat of dripping before
   serving. Make gravy in the usual way.

Baked Cod

Serves 2 (halve quantities for one person)

Oven temperature: 400°F, gas mark 6

Cooking time: 25 minutes

INGREDIENTS

a 7-oz. pkt. Birds Eye cod   2 oz. white breadcrumbs
  steaks, or fresh cod steaks   one and a half oz. of grated
salt and pepper   cheese
2 tomatoes, sliced

METHOD

1 Grease an ovenproof dish.
2 Place the fish steaks in the dish and season well.
3 Cover with sliced tomato – you may prefer to skin them first, see page 113.
4 Mix the breadcrumbs and cheese together and spread the mixture over the dish.
5 Bake at oven temperature 400°F, gas mark 6 for 25 minutes.

Baked Potatoes in Their Jackets

Oven temperature: 400°F–425°F, gas mark 6–7

Cooking time: 40 minutes to 1 hour

INGREDIENTS

even-sized, unblemished   a little butter or margarine
  potatoes

METHOD

1 Choose one medium-sized (4–6 oz.) potato per person.
2 Scrub well and dry.
3 Prick all over, through the skin, with a fork.
4 Rub the skin with butter or margarine, using grease-proof paper or the wrapping paper from the fat to avoid messy handling. This makes the skin delicious to eat.

5 Place on a baking tray or direct on the oven shelf, and
   bake at 400–425°F, gas mark 6–7 for 40 minutes to
   1 hour, according to size. When ready, they feel soft
   if squeezed gently with a cloth.
6 Cut lengthwise in halves and mash in plenty of
   butter and a little salt.

Beef Loaf

It is a real problem to find a small enough joint of meat
for one person. This is an excellent alternative; it gives
you a roast meat dinner which can be served with roast
potatoes, your favourite vegetables and gravy – and
there is no wastage through bones or fat.

Serves 2, or 1 hot serving, 1 cold serving next day

Oven temperature: 350°F, gas mark 4

Cooking time: 1 hour

INGREDIENTS

half a lb. raw minced beef
2 oz. fat bacon, minced (or
    snipped small with sharp
    scissors)
1–2 tablespoons Quick
    Quaker or similar oats,
    or 1 diced cooked medium-
    size potato

1 rounded tablespoon
    chutney
salt and pepper
1 egg
a little flour
parsley to garnish
tomato sauce (see page 114)
    or tomato ketchup

METHOD

1 With a spoon and fork (to avoid messy handling) put the minced beef into a bowl.
2 Add the bacon, oats or potato, chutney and seasoning.
3 Add a whole egg and fork it well in. Add a little flour – but the mixture needs to be soft.
4 *Either* press into a small loaf tin
   or grease a strip of greaseproof paper and wrap it round the roll to hold it in shape, then wrap it in kitchen foil and put onto a baking tray.
5 Bake for 1 hour at 350°F, gas mark 4 just above the centre of the oven.
6 Cut in 2–4 pieces and lift carefully onto a dish. Garnish with parsley and serve with tomato sauce or ketchup.

Blackcurrant Pudding

The creaminess of this pudding contrasts pleasantly with the sharpness of the blackcurrants. A quick way to serve plenty of nourishment.

Serves 2

Cooking time: a few minutes

INGREDIENTS

1 small can blackcurrants   a 5-oz. carton plain yogurt
a quarter of a packet   1 tablespoon lemon juice
  blackcurrant jelly

METHOD

1 Drain fruit and retain juice.
2 Dissolve jelly in heated fruit juice. Allow to cool
   slightly.
3 Whisk this with the yogurt and lemon juice.
4 Allow partially to set, mix in fruit and turn into
   serving dish. Serve cold.

Carrots (or Parsnips) Cooked in Butter

This is not only one of the tastiest ways of cooking
carrots, or parsnips, but also the most sensible – unless of
course you are on a fat-free diet. Root vegetables easily
absorb fat. By cooking not in water but in butter, you
help to conserve nourishment.

Cooking time: sliced old carrots or parsnips – 10–20
minutes
whole new carrots – up to 45 minutes

You need a thick saucepan with a really tight-fitting lid.
(This is essential because the vegetables cook in the

steam from their own moisture, and they produce so little steam that none of it must escape.)

If the lid of your saucepan does not fit tightly, use instead an enamel plate with weights on top to keep it down or an improvised lid of kitchen foil.

INGREDIENTS

carrots or parsnips
a large knob of butter
seasoning

a pinch of sugar
chopped parsley (optional)

METHOD

1 Scrub and scrape or peel the carrots and cut older carrots into even slices, not too thick. New carrots can be left whole. Parsnips need to be peeled and sliced.
2 Heat sufficient butter to cover well the bottom of the pan. When it is hot but not smoking, add the carrots or parsnips.
3 Add salt and pepper, but not too much because none of its flavour will be lost.
4 Cover with lid and cook over a *gentle* heat, shaking the pan occasionally so that the vegetables do not stick or burn. Sliced carrots or parsnips will take 10–20 minutes to become tender according to thickness. Whole new carrots may take up to 45 minutes.
5 Sprinkle with a good pinch of granulated or castor sugar – this helps to bring out the natural flavour of the vegetable. Also sprinkle with coarsely chopped parsley if you like the extra colour and flavour.
6 Serve with any buttery juices still remaining.

Carrots and Leeks

Serves 2

Cooking time: approximately 20–30 minutes, according to size

INGREDIENTS

2 large carrots or 4 smaller
  carrots, scraped or peeled
2 leeks
1 oz. margarine or butter
1 oz. plain flour, sieved

quarter of a pint of milk
quarter of a pint of vegetable
  water drained from the
  cooked carrots and leeks
seasoning

METHOD

1 Wash the prepared carrots. Leeks are generally gritty and muddy. The easiest way to prepare them is to cut off the roots, then cut the leeks lengthwise in half. Wash them under running cold water, freeing the mud with your fingers as gently as possible to keep the leeks from falling apart. Give a final soak in cold water to make sure they are really free from grit.

2 Slice the carrots and leeks fairly thickly.

3 Boil together in lightly-salted water till tender.

4 Drain off the cooking water into a bowl.

5 Into the pan with the drained carrots and leeks put the margarine, and when that has melted add the flour and half a pint of milk and vegetable water mixed.

6 Bring to the boil, stirring continuously, over low-medium heat. Allow the sauce to boil gently for about 3 minutes.

7 Adjust seasoning to taste before serving.

Note. Other vegetables can be cooked together in one pan, drained and then mashed together with a little margarine or butter and seasoning; you may find this simpler than making the sauce as above. Try a mixture of

potato and parsnip

or

potato and swede

Celery (or Leeks), Braised

Cooking time: 30 minutes

INGREDIENTS

a large knob of butter or margarine (approximately 1–2 oz.)
head of celery

a quarter of a chicken stock cube
approximately half a pint of water

METHOD

1 Cut off the root of the celery to separate the stalks. Discard any very tough or discoloured outside stalks and the outer leaves. Scrub and rinse the rest of the stalks, leaving on the small tender inner leaves if you like.

2 Cut into pieces about one inch long.

3   Melt the fat in the saucepan. Gently fry the celery
    in it for a few minutes, stirring occasionally. This
    helps to bring out the flavour.
4   Add the water and chicken stock cube, bring to the
    boil and simmer gently with the lid on the pan until
    the celery is softened, approximately 30 minutes (but
    it can be left a little longer if you wish). There is no
    need for further seasoning because the celery and the
    stock cube are both well flavoured.
5   Serve with the liquid from the pan which acts as a
    delicious gravy.

Note. Washed and cut up leeks can be cooked in
exactly the same way. For preparation of leeks, see
page 54.

Cheese and Cress Omelette

Serves 1

INGREDIENTS

2 eggs
1 tablespoon water
salt and pepper
half an oz. of butter
one and a half oz. of Cheddar
    cheese (sliced, then broken
    in pieces)

2–3 sprigs of watercress
    (roughly cut up with
    scissors) or some mustard
    and cress* (cut with
    scissors)

* Nowadays this is generally bought as 'growing cress' so
that a little can be cut off at a time, and the rest will keep fresh.

METHOD

1 Beat eggs, water and seasoning together in a small basin.

2 Heat butter in an omelette pan, or small frying-pan, and pour egg mixture into it.

3 Cook quickly, drawing the outside cooked mixture towards centre with a fork. Then tilt pan so that uncooked mixture goes to the edge (it is easiest at this stage to use a palette knife to lift the edges of the omelette).

4 Cook until top is creamy, then place cheese and cress over half the omelette furthest from handle.

5 Fold other half of omelette over filling and tip omelette out on to serving plate.

6 Serve immediately.

Cheese Crumb Chicken

Serves 2

Oven temperature: 400°F, gas mark 6

Cooking time: 1 hour

INGREDIENTS

2 chicken joints
2 oz. butter or margarine
1 oz. (2 heaped tablespoons) Quick Quaker or similar oats

2 heaped tablespoons grated Cheddar cheese
half a teaspoon salt
a little garlic powder, if liked

METHOD

1   Melt the butter or margarine in a shallow baking tin.
2   Mix together the oats, cheese, salt and garlic powder.
3   Dip the chicken joints into the melted butter, and
    then coat each thoroughly with the oat mixture.
4   Arrange joints in the baking tin and baste with the
    remaining butter or margarine.
5   Bake uncovered on the middle shelf, at 400°F, gas
    mark 6 for 1 hour.

Can be served with a fresh green salad, and potatoes
baked in their jackets.

Cheese and Marmite Bread and Butter Pudding

The recipe for a sweet bread and butter pudding can be
found in most general cookery books. So we are giving
for a change a more nourishing version for those of you
who may prefer savoury to sweet.

Serves 2

Oven temperature: 350°F, gas mark 4

Cooking time: 35–40 minutes

INGREDIENTS

2 large slices of bread and
  butter, crusts removed
a little Marmite
4 oz. grated cheese – a mild
  Cheddar

1 large egg
quarter of a pint of milk
salt and pepper
a pinch of dry mustard

METHOD

1   Place 1 slice of buttered bread, spread with Marmite,
    in the base of a greased small pie dish.

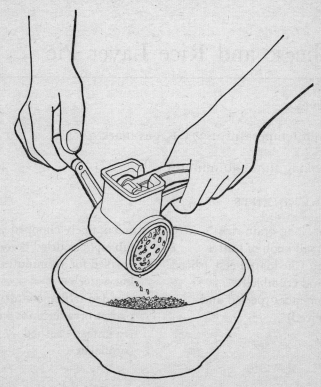

2   Add a layer of cheese, the remaining slice of buttered
     bread and finish with another layer of cheese.
3   Beat egg into milk – which you season with just a little
     salt, pepper and mustard – and strain over the pud-
     ding.
4   Bake in a moderate oven 350°F, gas mark 4 for 35–40
     minutes.
     Serve immediately.

Cheese and Rice Layer Pie

Serves 2

Oven temperature: 375°F, gas mark 5

Cooking time: 30 minutes

INGREDIENTS

2 oz. long-grain rice
a small knob of butter
4 oz. Cheddar cheese (sliced
and crumbled)
2 tomatoes (peeled and
sliced)

1 onion, finely chopped *or* 2
tablespoons dried onion
(soaked for 15 minutes in
hot water)
1 rounded tablespoon dry or
packet breadcrumbs – or
try instead crushed
cornflakes

METHOD

1 Boil the rice in well-salted water till softened. Drain.
2 Lightly butter the base of a small pie dish.
3 Put rice in the base of the dish.
4 Arrange half the cheese on top of the rice.
5 Put the tomato and onion in next, and finally top
   with remaining cheese.
6 Sprinkle the breadcrumbs or cornflakes over the pie.
7 Bake in a moderately hot oven (375°F, gas mark 5)
   for about 30 minutes.

Cheese Soufflé, One-stage

Serves 2

Oven temperature: 375°F, gas mark 5

Cooking time: 20–25 minutes (time depending on size of
dish)

INGREDIENTS

One-stage sauce

1 oz. *soft*, easy-creaming
   margarine
quarter of a pint of milk
1 oz. plain flour, sieved
salt and pepper
a pinch of dry mustard

To finish soufflé

2 standard eggs, separated
3 oz. Cheddar cheese, finely
   grated

METHOD

1 Place all sauce ingredients in a medium saucepan and bring to the boil, whisking all the time with a flat whisk; cook for 2–3 minutes. Cool slightly.

2 Beat egg yolks into this sauce, and add the cheese.

3 With a clean beater, whisk the egg whites stiffly.

4 Cut and fold the whites into the sauce until the soufflé is evenly mixed (it is easiest to do this with a metal tablespoon).

5 Pour into a greased one-and-a-half to two-pint oven-proof dish which will allow room for the mixture to rise (preferably a soufflé case with straight sides) and bake on the middle shelf of a pre-heated oven, 375°F, gas mark 5, for 20–25 minutes, according to the size of the dish.

6 Serve immediately.

Chicken Casserole

Serves 1

Cooking time: 40 minutes

INGREDIENTS

1 oz. margarine
1 chicken portion
1 small onion, sliced, or 1 tablespoon dried onion

1–2 oz. mushrooms, sliced (if you buy quarter of a lb. mushrooms, use the rest for mushroom omelette or for mushrooms on toast)

1 tomato, quartered

quarter of a pint stock (or
quarter of a cube of
chicken stock dissolved in
water)

2 teaspoons tomato puree

salt and pepper (optional)

METHOD

1   Take a saucepan with a lid, heat margarine and fry
chicken and onion (if using fresh) for 8–10 minutes.
Pour off the fat. This can be used for other frying.

2   Add remaining ingredients (if using dried onion,
include at this stage).

3   Stir well, bring to the boil and simmer with the lid on
for 30 minutes. Check flavour and add seasoning if
necessary. You may find sufficient flavour has been
provided by the stock cube.

Chops and Onions

Serves 1

Cooking time: approximately 15 minutes for thin cutlets, anything up to about 35 minutes for a thick chop

INGREDIENTS

butter or margarine

a tablespoon of flour, mixed
with a little salt and pepper

1 lamb chop or 2 small
cutlets

1 small to medium onion,
peeled and sliced

METHOD

1   If using thin cutlets, start frying the sliced onion in
    the pan first – it will take about 20 minutes to soften
    and turn golden.
2   To fry the chop or cutlets: wash and pat dry
    with kitchen paper, and dust with the seasoned
    flour.
    Fry in the same pan, turning the meat over occasion-
    ally until it is cooked well through and beginning to
    crisp and brown. (Most people like lamb well done
    in the middle so that a skewer or sharp knife pushed
    into the centre will not bring out a fluid too red
    or pink.) A fairly thick chop may take about 35
    minutes to fry, a thin cutlet may only take about 15
    minutes.
3   Remove the chop or cutlets on to the plate and keep
    warm.
4   Very carefully pour into the pan of onions just a little
    water.
5   Stir it around, bring to the boil and you will have
    plump onions in a lovely golden buttery liquor to
    pour over the chop.

   Note. These plump buttery onions are also delicious
poured over fried steak or liver or – far less expensive –
beefburgers.

Cod Charlotte

Comment from Harlow Technical College: 'No difficulty at all, and all liked the crispy cubes of bread on top of the fish. We served frozen peas with this, with the Lemon Sponge Pudding (see page 140) to follow.'

Serves 2

Oven temperature: 350°F, gas mark 4

Cooking time: 35–40 minutes

INGREDIENTS

a 7-oz. packet of Birds Eye cod steaks, or unfrozen cod steaks
2 eggs
quarter of a pint of milk
1 tablespoon chopped parsley (it is easiest to snip the parsley roughly with kitchen scissors)

salt and pepper
3 slices of bread about half an inch thick, crusts removed
about one and a half oz. of margarine

METHOD

1   Place the cod steaks in a greased ovenproof dish.
2   Beat together the eggs and milk and add parsley and seasoning. Pour over the fish.
3   Cut the slices of bread into half-inch cubes.
4   Melt the margarine in a pan, add the bread cubes, and toss until coated.

5   Cover the fish with the bread cubes, and bake in a
     moderate oven 350°F, gas mark 4 for 35–40 minutes.

Cottage Pie

Serves 2

INGREDIENTS

half a lb. raw minced beef   mashed potato for topping
2 tablespoons condensed
   soup (the best to use is
   oxtail, kidney or
   mulligatawny)

METHOD

1   In a saucepan, stir minced beef with a fork over low
     heat until lightly brown, about 10 minutes—there is
     sufficient fat in the mince to allow it to cook in this
     way.
2   Pour the condensed soup over the meat and mix well.
     Simmer for a further 10 minutes over low heat.
3   Put into a flameproof pie dish and cover with mashed
     potato.
4   Place under a hot grill until browned.

Note. Instead of raw minced beef, cooked beef or lamb
may be used; cut up finely, this need not be cooked in

fat but mixed with the soup only. Reconstituted packet
potato may be used to cover top of pie. Keep the
remainder of the tin of soup in a cold place, dilute and
heat up for a meal the following day.

Curry Sauce

An economical way of 'stretching' cooked meat, fish,
vegetables or eggs to make a substantial meal. Serves
2–3, can be reheated next day, so make it for 2 meals
if you are living on your own.

Cooking time: 30–45 minutes

INGREDIENTS

a small knob of margarine
1 small onion, finely chopped
1 small sharp eating apple,
  peeled and finely chopped
1–2 level teaspoons curry
  powder
1 rounded tablespoon plain
  flour

half a pint of stock
1 teaspoon chutney
1 level teaspoon jam or
  marmalade
a few sultanas
salt and pepper
1 teaspoon vinegar or lemon
  juice

METHOD

1 In a saucepan, melt the margarine and fry the onion,
   apple and curry powder together for 2–3 minutes.
2 Add all the remaining ingredients except the vinegar

or lemon juice and, stirring continuously with a wooden spoon, bring to the boil. Cover and simmer gently for 30–45 minutes.

3   Add vinegar or lemon juice just before serving.

Serve with hard-boiled eggs, or with diced cooked meat, chicken, fish or vegetables. (Put into the curry sauce, bring to the boil, and simmer till hot – allow at least 15 minutes for cooked meat.)

Devilled Kidneys

Serves 1

Cooking time: 10 minutes

INGREDIENTS

2 lamb's kidneys
a knob of butter
1 rasher of bacon
1 slice of toast
tomato or other vegetable

1 teaspoon vinegar
1 small flat teaspoon of
  made mustard
a sprinkling of pepper and
  salt

METHOD

1   Cut the kidneys in half and, with pointed scissors, remove the inner core and then peel off the skin.

2   Fry the halved kidneys gently in butter for 8 minutes, turning them once or twice.

3   Meanwhile, start grilling the bacon (and tomato, if you like it cooked) and making the toast.

4   Stir the vinegar, mustard, pepper and salt into the kidney pan. Cook 2 minutes more.
5   Serve on toast with bacon and tomato or other vegetable.

Ena's Austrian Biscuits

For 2 dozen biscuits – these keep well in an airtight tin.

Oven temperature: 400°F, gas mark 6

Cooking time: approximately 15 minutes

INGREDIENTS

Pastry

a quarter lb. of fresh unsalted butter

a quarter lb. curd cheese, or sieved cottage cheese
a quarter lb. plain flour

Filling

apricot jam

a few seedless raisins

Icing

1–2 oz. icing sugar, sieved

a few drops of lemon juice

METHOD

1   Press all pastry ingredients together with a wooden spoon. Using the hand, knead to a dough.
2   Roll out into an oblong approximately 9 inches by 12 inches.
3   Spread with apricot jam, sprinkle with a few seedless raisins and roll up lengthwise like a swiss roll.

4 Cut obliquely about half an inch thick and place on a baking tray, allowing a little space for spreading.
5 Bake in a fairly hot oven, 400°F, gas mark 6 for about 15 minutes, or until golden.
6 As they are cooling, ice with sieved icing sugar mixed with lemon juice to a glacé-icing consistency.

Fisherman's Pudding

Serves 2–3

Oven temperature: 375°F, gas mark 5

Cooking time: 1 hour, 30 minutes

We wondered whether this recipe might seem too troublesome. But, when tried out at Almondbury Further Education Centre, 16 students tried it, all 16 said they liked it very much and all 16 said they wanted to cook it again at home. So here it is:

INGREDIENTS

8 oz. fillet of white fish
4 tablespoons milk
4 small slices white bread, broken into small pieces

2 oz. packet of shredded suet
salt and pepper
1 tablespoon parsley, chopped
1 egg, beaten

METHOD

1 Place fish fillet in baking tin with the milk. Bake, covered, for 20 minutes at 375°F, gas mark 5.

2 Remove skin, flake the fish and combine with remaining ingredients, together with the fish liquor.

3 Transfer to a greased 1-pint pudding basin, cover securely with greaseproof paper, or foil, and steam for 1 hour, 30 minutes.

4 Can be served with white sauce and vegetables.

Fricassée of Chicken in One Pan

Serves 2

Cooking time: 8–10 minutes   *copied in book*

INGREDIENTS

1 oz. margarine
1 small onion, peeled, chopped or sliced

2 oz. mushrooms, washed and sliced

1 oz. margarine
1 oz. plain flour

half a pint of milk
salt and pepper to taste

about 6 oz. cooked chicken, cut into small pieces
small can of peas, drained

a slice of white bread, toasted and cut into fingers
wedges of lemon

METHOD

1 Melt 1 oz. margarine in saucepan and fry onion and mushrooms until softened but not browned.

2 *To make sauce* add the next ounce of margarine, with the flour, milk and seasoning, to the pan of onions

and mushrooms. Whisking all the time with a balloon whisk, bring to the boil and cook 2–3 minutes. (It is possible to whisk vigorously with a fork, but it is less tiring and more efficient to use a balloon whisk.)

3   Add the chicken and peas and reheat.
4   Pour into serving dish or onto plates and garnish with fingers of toast and wedges of lemon. (For a delicious flavour, squeeze the lemon into the fricassée before eating.)

Fruity Pan Pudding

Serves 4.   2 servings one day, reheated the second day*

Cooking time: 30 minutes

You will need a small (2-pint) saucepan with a tightly fitting lid.

INGREDIENTS

a 10 or 15 oz. can of fruit,   4 tablespoons water
  e.g. plums, cherries

* To reheat on the second day, it is best to break up the suet crust like small dumplings so that they will heat through quickly. You may find it necessary to add more liquid, e.g. water flavoured with vitamin C blackcurrant drink.

Pastry

3 oz. self-raising flour
3 rounded tablespoons of
  packet shredded suet
pinch of salt
1 oz. castor sugar

a quarter of a teaspoon
  ground cinnamon or mixed
  spice (optional)
about 3 tablespoons milk to
  mix

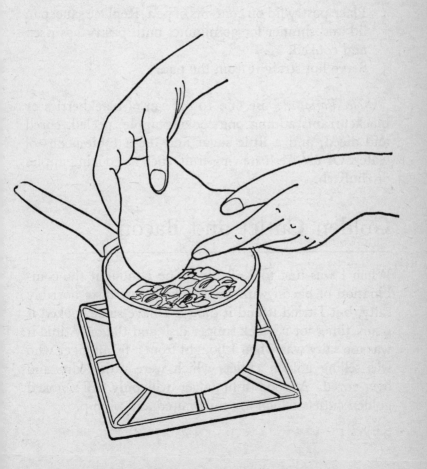

METHOD

1   Place the stoned fruit with its juice with the extra water in a saucepan and heat to simmering point.
2   Mix together pastry ingredients to form a firm dough.
3   Roll or pat out pastry to a circle the size of the top of the pan.
4   Place pastry lid on contents of pan. Replace saucepan lid and simmer for 30 minutes until pastry has risen and cooked.
5   Serve hot straight from the pan.

Note. Variation: use one 10 oz. can of blackberries or blackcurrants adding one cooking apple, peeled, cored and diced, and a little sugar and the 4 tablespoons of water. Or use fresh stewing fruit, such as cooking apples or rhubarb.

Golden Cutlet and Bacon

When I was first told of this recipe I thought the combination of bacon with smoked fish must taste horribly salty, but I tried it and it didn't. I have since cooked it many times for a quick supper dish and the only time it was too salty was when I bought from a fishmonger who was selling golden cutlets which were rather dry and over-cured. A good fishmonger will only sell smoked golden cutlets which are mild-cured and plump.

Serves 1

INGREDIENTS

1 smoked golden cutlet   1 rasher of streaky bacon

METHOD

1   Grill the golden cutlet (without any addition of fat or seasoning), skin-side down, under medium heat until the escape of a small ooze of milky white fluid tells you that it is practically cooked. (This will probably only take about 5 minutes.)

2   Cut out any small bone from the bacon, remove the rind, then lay the bacon on top of the fish.

3   Continue grilling until the bacon is cooked and, if you like, just beginning to crisp at the edges. Eat the fish and bacon together, just looking out for a very few small bones sometimes left in the fish.

Grilled Cod

Serves 1 or 2

Cooking time: approximately 15 minutes

INGREDIENTS

2 cod cutlets (or 1 cutlet per person) and a little margarine

1 oz. Cheddar cheese
1 oz. margarine
seasoning
a little milk

METHOD

1   Place the cod cutlet, dotted with a little margarine,
    on the greased grill pan, and cook under a medium
    grill for about 5 or 6 minutes, according to the thick-
    ness of the cutlet.
2   Grate or crumble the cheese and mix with the 1 oz.
    margarine, the seasoning and a little milk, until it is
    of spreading consistency.
3   Remove cutlet from under grill. Turn the fish over
    and spread with the cheese mixture.
4   Grill gently for a further 6–10 minutes.

Lancashire Hot-pot

Serves 2, or one serving one day, *thoroughly* reheated for
second serving next day. Cooked in oven or on top of
stove depending on rest of meal

Oven temperature: 350°F, gas mark 4

Cooking time: 1 hour, 30 minutes

INGREDIENTS

4 pieces neck of lamb   1 teaspoon Bovril
1 medium onion   quarter of a pint of water
1 carrot   seasoning
2 medium potatoes   a little chopped parsley
piece of celery, if available   (optional)
piece of turnip (optional)

METHOD

1   Wash the meat.
2   Prepare vegetables and cut up small, except for one
    potato.
3   Place vegetables and meat in layers in casserole or
    saucepan and add seasoning.
4   Dissolve Bovril in hot water and add to the meat and
    vegetables.
5   Slice the remaining potato thinly and arrange on top.
    Cover casserole or pan with lid.
6   *For cooking on top of the stove:*
    Bring pan to the boil, reduce heat to the lowest and
    simmer for 1 hour, 30 minutes.

    For Cooking in the Oven:

    Place casserole in oven 350°F, gas mark 4 for 45
    minutes. Remove from oven, remove lid, and brush
    potatoes with melted fat, leave lid off and cook for at
    least a further 45 minutes.
7   Serve sprinkled with chopped parsley.

Note. If you live alone eat half and cool the remaining
portion *quickly*. Reheat thoroughly the following day in
the saucepan or replace the casserole without the lid in
the oven and bake at 350°F, gas mark 4 for 30 minutes.

Lemon Cake

Oven temperature: 350°F, gas mark 4

Cooking time: approximately 45 minutes

INGREDIENTS

Cake

4 oz. Stork or similar
    soft margarine

4 oz. castor sugar

2 eggs, large

1 tablespoon milk

4 oz. self-raising
    flour   } sieved

1 level teaspoon } together
    baking powder }

grated rind of 1 lemon

Lemon Syrup

2 oz. castor sugar

juice of 1 lemon

METHOD

1 Grease and line the base of a 7-inch cake tin using greased greaseproof paper or ungreased Bakewell non-stick paper.

2 Place all cake ingredients in mixing bowl and beat with a wooden spoon until the mixture is smooth, 2–3 minutes.

3 Place in cake tin and bake on the middle shelf of a moderate oven, 350°F, gas mark 4 for approximately 45 minutes.

4 When cake is baked – when it is firm to a light finger-touch, and just shrunk away from the side of the tin – turn it out on to the cooling tray and leave upside-down.

5   Make lemon syrup by dissolving castor sugar in the
    juice of the lemon over gentle heat and boiling it for
    one minute.
6   With the bottom of the cake uppermost, make three
    or four slits with a sharp knife, and pour the warm
    syrup into the warm cake.
7   When cool, reverse the cake and dust with sieved
    icing sugar.

Lemon Pudding

Serves 2–3

Cooking time: 2 hours to 2 hours, 30 minutes

You need a small (1-pint) pudding basin

INGREDIENTS

4 oz. self-raising flour   1 lemon – juicy and thin-
2 oz. of packet shredded suet   skinned
pinch salt   3 tablespoons golden syrup
milk for mixing

METHOD

1   Mix together flour, suet and salt.
2   Add sufficient milk to make a firm dough.
3   Roll out three quarters of the dough and line a
    greased 1-pint pudding basin.
4   Grate lemon rind and mix with syrup.
5   Discard pith from lemon.

6   Place whole lemon in the centre of the basin.
7   Surround with syrup and place suet-crust lid on top,
     sealing edges firmly (first damp with a little water to
     make edges easy to seal).
8   Cover securely with foil and steam or boil for 2 hours
     to 2 hours 30 minutes.

Note. The lemon disintegrates during cooking, making
a gorgeously tangy, syrupy pudding.

Liver and Bacon Bake

Serves 2 (or halve quantities for one serving)

Oven temperature: 350°F, gas mark 4

Cooking time: 45 minutes

INGREDIENTS

2 slices of lamb's or pig's
  liver
stock made with a little
  Marmite or Bovril

packet stuffing, e.g. Paxo
  Lemon Stuffing – (2
  tablespoons stuffing with 4
  tablespoons boiling water)
4 rashers streaky bacon

METHOD

1   Put the liver in an ovenproof dish.
2   Barely cover with the Marmite or Bovril stock.
3   Make up 2 tablespoons stuffing as directed on the
     packet.

4 Spread the stuffing on top of the liver.
5 Top with the bacon rashers.
6 Bake uncovered in a moderate oven 350°F, gas mark
   4 for 45 minutes.

Macaroni, Italian Style

Serves 2

Oven temperature: 375°F, gas mark 5

Cooking time: approximately 35 minutes, including
cooking of macaroni

INGREDIENTS

2 oz. quick-cooking macaroni   salt and pepper
8-oz. can tomatoes   4 oz. grated or sliced and
2 oz. sliced ham (in small   crumbled Cheddar cheese
  pieces)*

METHOD

1 Cook macaroni in boiling salted water for 7 minutes,
   or as directed on packet. Drain.
2 Mix macaroni, tomatoes, ham and seasoning
   together. Turn into a shallow three-quarter pint
   ovenproof dish or a deep pie plate six and a half
   inches in diameter.

  * Comment from Charles Keene College of Further Education: suggest grilled bacon or the end of a bacon joint as
cheaper alternatives to sliced ham.

3   Top with grated or sliced and crumbled cheese.
4   Cook in a moderately hot oven 375°F, gas mark 5 for
    about 25 minutes.

Meat Balls

Serves 1

Cooking time: 1 hour

INGREDIENTS

a quarter lb. of minced beef   half an egg*
half a slice of bread with   a little flour
    crust removed   dripping
salt and pepper and nutmeg   1 small onion, finely chopped
chopped parsley or dried   stock or – better still –
    parsley (optional)   canned tomato juice

METHOD

1   In a bowl, break up minced meat with a fork.
2   Soak bread in water for a minute or two, then squeeze
    it as dry as possible and fork it into the meat. Season
    well with salt, pepper, nutmeg and chopped parsley.

   * Use the other half to add to scrambled egg, or make
Lazy Soup (see page 23).

3   Beat egg lightly and add to the mixture, mixing very
    well. Form into 3 small cakes and dip in flour.
4   Heat some dripping in a saucepan and fry the meat
    balls on both sides until browned on the outside.
5   Remove from the pan and in the same fat lightly fry
    the chopped onion. Sprinkle over this a dessertspoon
    of flour and mix well.
6   Return meat to pan and pour in stock or tomato juice
    almost to cover meat, add a little salt and simmer,
    covered, for an hour.

To serve 2, or to make enough for 2 days for 1 person:

Double the above quantities
or
Use quarter of a lb. of minced beef and quarter of a lb.
of minced pork in place of half a lb. of minced beef.
    If you are saving half to reheat next day, follow these
hygienic rules:

1   Straight away cool the hot meat balls and sauce
    rapidly by running cold water over the covered pan
    and stirring the contents of the pan occasionally till
    cold. Keep cold and covered.
2   Next day reheat *thoroughly* (cut the meat balls in
    halves or quarters if you wish to make sure they are
    hot all the way through).

Meat Stew, Norwegian Style

Serves 2 – or one serving one day, the second serving next day.

Cooking time: 1 hour, 30 minutes

You will need a medium-sized saucepan with a tightly fitting lid.

INGREDIENTS

half a pound of stewing
  steak
half a cabbage, coarsely
  shredded

half a pound of carrots,
  peeled and sliced
salt and pepper
flour
chopped parsley (optional)

METHOD

1 Cut the stewing steak into fairly large cubes (the butcher may do this for you).
2 Using a medium-sized saucepan with a tightly-fitting lid put in:
   (a) a layer of cabbage and carrots
   (b) a little seasoning and a good sprinkling of flour
   (c) a few pieces of meat
   (d) a little seasoning and a good sprinkling of flour.
3 Continue to add layers of vegetables and meat, sprinkling each layer with seasoning and flour.
4 When all the meat and vegetables have been used up, less than half-cover with water.
5 Put the lid on the pan and simmer for about 1 hour, 30 minutes.

6   Serve sprinkled with parsley if you like.
    This is just as good – if not better – thoroughly
    reheated again for a second meal next day.

Note. For a cheaper stew, instead of the stewing steak
use a *meaty breast of lamb*, well trimmed of excess fat and
cut into good-sized strips. (The butcher may first bone
this for you; if not, ask him to chop it so that you can cut
it easily into strips, and cook it with the bones in.) This
lamb and cabbage stew is particularly popular in
Norway.

Meringue Rice

Cooked in the oven or on top of the stove, depending on the rest of the meal.

Serves 2

Oven temperature: 400°F, gas mark 6

Cooking time: 8–10 minutes

INGREDIENTS

1 small tin of rice pudding or
   any other tinned milk
   pudding, or home-made

a little sharp-flavoured
   stewed or canned fruit (the
   rest may be used for fruit
   salad for another meal,
   some fresh fruit may be
   added to it)
1 egg white
2 tablespoons castor sugar

METHOD

1   Put milk pudding into a fireproof dish – if grilling,
    avoid using a glass dish. Lay the drained fruit on top.
2   Whisk the egg white till stiff, add 1 tablespoon castor
    sugar, whisk again.
3   Fold in remaining castor sugar and pile on top of the
    pudding.
4   *Either* bake in a hot oven 400°F, gas mark 6 for 8–10
    minutes *or* put under a medium grill till golden brown.

Mushroom Soup

Serves 2

Cooking time: approximately 15 minutes

Note. Although there are packets and cans of mushroom
soup in the shops, the flavour of this home-made mushroom soup is so outstandingly good that we felt it worth
inclusion in this book.

INGREDIENTS

quarter of a pound of
   washed and finely chopped
   mushrooms
quarter of a pint of water
quarter of a chicken stock
   cube
half a pint of milk

1 oz. soft margarine
1 oz. plain flour, sieved
a pinch of mixed herbs
seasoning to taste
a little chopped parsley
   (optional)

METHOD

1   Cook the chopped mushrooms gently in the water
    with a quarter stock cube for 5–10 minutes.
2   Remove from heat, add the milk first and then
    all other ingredients, apart from seasoning and
    parsley.
3   Return the pan to the heat, and whisking continu-
    ously with a flat or balloon whisk, bring to the boil
    and cook for 2–3 minutes.
4   Season to taste, and serve, sprinkled with a little
    chopped parsley.

One-pot Kedgeree

This is a useful recipe if you have only one cooking ring,
or if you want to save fuel and washing up by using only
one pot. The method may sound complicated, but try
it; it is very easy.

Serves 2–3 (can be served hot one day, cold the
next)

   Or, for 1 person, halve quantities but cook all the
haddock and use half for Scrambled Haddock and Eggs
(see page 22) next day.

Cooking time: about 20 minutes

INGREDIENTS

a seven-and-a-half-ounce
   packet Birds Eye Boil-in-
   the-Bag Buttered Smoked
   Haddock
2 oz. long-grain rice
2 eggs, rinsed under the tap
   just before use

3–4 tablespoons salad cream
1 tablespoon chopped parsley
salt and pepper
lettuce leaves and tomato
   wedges (when served cold)

METHOD

1   Bring about 3 pints of water to the boil in a large
    pan, and place the boil-in-the-bag *fish*, the *rice*, and
    eggs (left in their shells) in the pan.
2   Return to the boil and simmer for 12 minutes.
3   Remove the eggs and run them under cold water.
    Simmer the fish and rice for a further 5 minutes.
4   Remove the bag of fish and allow to cool.
    Strain the rice.
5   Shell and chop or slice the eggs.
    Remove the fish from the bag, but do not throw away
    the liquor.
    Skin and flake the fish.
    Mix eggs and fish with the rice.
    Add the liquor from the bag.
6   Add the salad cream and parsley and season to
    taste.
7   Good hot or cold.
    Serve without garnish when hot.
    Serve with lettuce leaves and tomato wedges when
    cold.

Orange Cabinet-pudding

Serves 2 – or 1 serving hot, 1 serving cold next day

Oven temperature: 350°F, gas mark 4

Cooking time: approximately 25 minutes

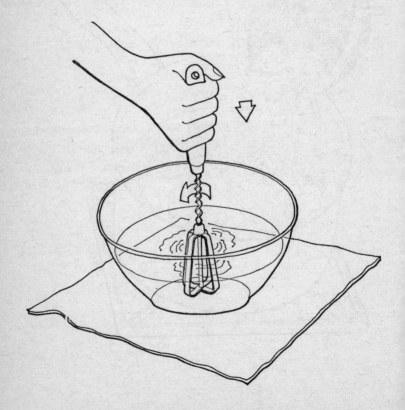

INGREDIENTS

one and a half trifle sponge
    cakes, cut in half
4 glacé cherries, cut in half
a few sultanas
either
one and a half tablespoons
    frozen orange juice,
    thawed and

one and a half tablespoons
    water
or
the juice of 1 medium orange

quarter of a pint of milk
1 large egg (beaten)
1 tablespoon sugar

METHOD

1 Place the sponge cakes in a small greased ovenproof
   dish and sprinkle with glacé cherries and sultanas.
2 Beat together the orange juice, water (if used), milk
   and egg, and add the sugar.
3 Pour over the sponge cakes and place the dish in an
   oven, 350°F, gas mark 4 for approximately 25
   minutes or until set.

Note. Add a topping of cream to this when cold and
you turn it into a trifle.

Pilaff

Serves 1–2

Small pieces of cooked rabbit, lean lamb or chicken can
be turned into an attractive pilaff.

INGREDIENTS

1 large tomato with skin removed (dip tomato into a pan of boiling water for less than a minute, put under cold water to make it easy to handle; the skin slips off easily)

1 oz. margarine

2 oz. long-grain rice

half a teacup stock (may be made with vegetable extract or stock cube)

half a teacup milk

1 teacup diced cooked rabbit, lamb or chicken

seasoning

standard egg, beaten

METHOD

1   Fry the sliced tomato in the margarine.
2   Add rice and toss for a minute or so in the tomato mixture.
3   Add stock and milk, and bring slowly to the boil, stirring well. Cook gently until rice is nearly soft. Add meat and seasoning and heat gently.
4   Just before serving stir in the beaten egg.

Poached Sausages

Comment from testers: 'We'll have this again and again! A delicious way of cooking sausages. In our opinion, far more digestible than frying.'

Serves 2

Cooking time: 25 minutes

INGREDIENTS

half a pound of pork
  sausages
half a pint of milk
1 bay leaf
1 small onion, sliced, or 1
  tablespoon dried onion

salt and pepper
1 oz. margarine or butter
1 oz. plain flour
1–2 teaspoon chopped capers
  and/or 1 tablespoon
  parsley

METHOD

1 Very gently poach the sausages in the milk with the
bay leaf, onion and seasoning, for 20 minutes.

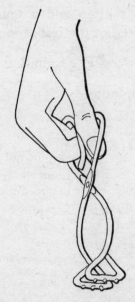

2 Remove sausages, place in the serving dish or on
plates, and keep warm.

3 Add the margarine or butter to the milk, then sift in

the flour. Return to the heat and, whisking continuously with a flat or balloon whisk, bring to the boil
and cook 2–3 minutes.
4 Add chopped capers, and/or the chopped parsley,
check the seasoning and pour over the sausages.

Pork and Apple Slices

Serves 2 – or use 1 chop and a small apple for one
serving, without altering the rest of the ingredients.

Oven temperature: 400°F, gas mark 6

Cooking time: 30 minutes

INGREDIENTS

2 pork chops
a pinch of salt
1 tablespoon lemon juice
half a teaspoon brown sugar
1 teaspoon dry mustard

a pinch of garlic powder, if
 liked
1 sliced medium cooking
 apple

METHOD

Baking

1 Trim chops, and place in a greased ovenproof dish.
2 Blend salt, lemon juice, sugar, mustard and garlic
   powder and pour over chops.

3 Bake in pre-heated hot oven, 400°F, gas mark 6 for
   15 minutes.
4 Top the chops with the apple slices, baste well and
   bake for a further 15 minutes.

METHOD 2

Grilling

1 Trim chops and place in a greased shallow small iron
   casserole or a flameproof Pyrosil Handipan, or the
   grill pan.
2 Heat the grill, lower the temperature to medium,
   grill chops for 15 minutes on one side. Remove from
   the heat and turn the chops.
3 Blend all the ingredients as above for method 1 and
   pour over the chops. Top with sliced apple, and
   return to heat for a further 15 minutes.
      Be sure the apple slices do not brown too fast;
   baste if required.

Potato Scones

Next time you are preparing mashed potatoes, you may
like to make some extra for these delicious Potato Scones.
   Serve hot, sliced and buttered for tea, or as a pudding
with golden syrup.

Makes 8

Oven temperature: 400°F, gas mark 6

Cooking time: 15 minutes

INGREDIENTS

4 oz. self-raising flour	1 tablespoon castor sugar
2 oz. of packet shredded suet	1 tablespoon currants
a pinch of salt	1 tablespoon sultanas
4 oz. cold mashed potato	milk for mixing

METHOD

1 Mix together all ingredients with sufficient milk to make a stiff dough.
2 Roll out to half an inch thick and cut out 8 rounds using a 2-inch plain cutter.
3 Brush with milk.
4 Place on greased baking sheet and bake at 400°F, gas mark 6 for about 15 minutes.

Quick Cabbage

The quick preparation, cooking and serving help to prevent loss of valuable vitamin C.

Serves 1–2

Cooking time: 5 minutes

INGREDIENTS

a piece of raw cabbage *	a large knob of butter or a
salt	little cooking oil

  * Note. This method is for an ordinary cooking cabbage. The firm salad cabbage is harder and is better shredded raw in a cole-slaw salad.

METHOD

1 Choose a small saucepan with a tightly fitting lid. If the lid does not fit well, use foil or an enamel plate, as recommended in the recipe for Carrots Cooked in Butter (see page 52).

2 Shred the cabbage *very* finely and wash it in a colander under running cold water.

3 Warm the butter or oil in the saucepan, using
   sufficient to cover the bottom of the pan when
   heated.
4 Add the cabbage, still wet from the colander. Shake
   in a little salt, but not too much because none of its
   flavour will be lost.
5 Cook *gently*, with the lid tightly on, for approximately
   5 minutes, shaking the pan occasionally to prevent
   sticking and burning. Serve at once with the buttery
   juice.

Quick Fish Soufflé

Serves 2

Oven temperature: 350°–375°F, gas mark 4–5

Cooking time: 20–30 minutes

INGREDIENTS

half a pound of cooked*   seasoning, tomato ketchup
   white fish   and mixed herbs
                                   2 eggs

METHOD

1 Separate eggs and beat the yolks into the hot flaked
   fish. Season with pepper and salt and flavour well with
   tomato ketchup and a good pinch of mixed herbs.
2 Whisk egg whites stiffly and fold into the fish mixture.

3 Pile into a buttered ovenproof dish, leaving room for soufflé to rise, and bake in a pre-heated oven 350°–375°F, gas mark 4–5, for 20–30 minutes, depending on the size of dish and the temperature used.

4 Serve, with extra tomato sauce if you like.

* To steam the fish: place on an enamel or other heatproof plate, dot with butter or margarine, moisten with a little milk, season with pepper and salt. Cover with an upturned plate, or the lid of a saucepan. Place the plate of fish on top of the saucepan, in which there are a few inches of gently simmering water – keep simmering on top of the stove. Make sure the plate is large enough to balance easily on top of the saucepan, and lift it off with oven gloves when the fish is cooked (when it is opaque and soft) to prevent scalding yourself in the steam from the pan.

Alternatively, as you will be using the oven later, you may prefer baking for the preliminary cooking of the fish.

To bake the fish: place in a baking tin with the butter or margarine, milk and seasoning, cover and bake for 20 minutes – or longer for a thick cut – at 375°F, gas mark 5.

Rhubarb Bread and Butter Pudding

Serves 2

Oven temperature: 350°F, gas mark 4

Cooking time: 40 minutes

INGREDIENTS

2 large slices of white bread and butter (crusts removed)

3 tablespoons stewed rhubarb pieces (well-drained) canned or fresh

a quarter pint of milk

1 large egg

1 tablespoon granulated sugar

METHOD

1 Grease a small pie dish, and arrange one slice of bread on the base, butter-side up.

2 Cover with the rhubarb pieces, adding sugar to taste for fresh rhubarb.

3 With a fork, mash and beat up the remaining slice of bread and butter with the beaten egg and milk, pour over the rhubarb, and sprinkle with 1 tablespoon granulated sugar.

4 Bake in a moderate oven, 350°F, gas mark 4 for 40 minutes.

This dish is good with custard or cream.

Rice Pudding

Round-grain pudding rice is generally a little cheaper than long-grain rice, but if you only have long-grain in the house you will find that it gives you just as good results in a sweet rice pudding as it does in savoury dishes.

Serves 2–3

Cooking time: 1 hour–1 hour, 30 minutes

INGREDIENTS

one and a half ounces of   1 pint milk
  round-grain or long-grain   2 oz. (four and a half heaped
  rice   tablespoons) Marvel, or
1 oz. sugar   similar milk powder
half an ounce of butter or
  margarine

SAUCEPAN METHOD

1   Put the rice, sugar, butter and milk in a saucepan.
2   Sprinkle in the Marvel, or similar milk powder, and
    stir well until it has dissolved.
3   Bring the milk and rice to the boil, cover the pan
    with a lid and simmer *gently* for 1 hour–1 hour, 30
    minutes. It is advisable to stir the rice from time to
    time.
4   Idea from Scandinavia: for a change, put some
    butter, sugar and cinnamon on the table. Add a knob
    of butter to the pudding then sprinkle generously
    with sugar and cinnamon before stirring and eating.
    Add more butter, sugar and cinnamon as desired.

OVEN METHOD

Serves 2–3

Oven temperature: 300°F, gas mark 2

Cooking time: 2 hours–2 hours, 15 minutes

1   Put the rice and sugar in a buttered ovenproof dish
    with the butter and milk. Add Marvel or similar
    milk powder and stir until it has dissolved.
2   Cook in a slow oven 300°F, gas mark 2 for 2 hours–
    2 hours, 15 minutes. Stir once or twice in the first
    one and a half hours. When ready the rice should be
    creamy, the milk nearly absorbed and the surface
    golden brown.

Note. The addition of a couple of ounces of Marvel or
other skimmed dried milk obviously adds to the normal
cost of a rice pudding, but by adding it to the pint of
milk already in the recipe you are packing in value for
money in terms of nourishment. We had many delighted
comments on the extra creaminess in flavour and texture.

Risotto

Risotto can equally well use up left-over cooked chicken,
beef or lamb. Several of the ingredients can be 'optional'.
For example, leave out the mushrooms or the bacon (or
substitute a slice of cooked ham); add cut up tomatoes
instead of peas, or else use a small can of vegetables.
Dried onion can replace the peeled, chopped fresh onion.
In other words, this is what I call a good-natured recipe –
it can be adapted to suit your larder.

Serves 2–3

Cooking time: 25 minutes

INGREDIENTS

1 oz. margarine
1 small onion, peeled and
  chopped (or use dried
  onion)
2 oz. mushrooms, washed and
  chopped
3 oz. long-grain rice
2 oz. streaky bacon, chopped

half a pint chicken stock,
  from steamed chicken (or
  water and half a stock
  cube)
salt and pepper, to taste
tomato puree, optional
1 small packet of peas
  (frozen or dried)
6 oz. cooked chicken, beef or
  lamb, cut into pieces

METHOD

1 Melt margarine and fry the chopped fresh onion (if used), mushrooms, rice and bacon for 5–8 minutes over gentle heat in a medium saucepan.
2 Add stock, dried onion (if used) and seasonings, stir well and bring to the boil and simmer with the lid on the pan for 20–25 minutes, adding a little tomato puree (optional) to give colour, and stirring occasionally.
3 Cook the peas separately, but do not overcook.
4 Meanwhile, stir in the chicken or other meat and thoroughly reheat. Add the peas. Serve hot.

Savoury Frits

Serves 1

Cooking time: approximately 15 minutes

INGREDIENTS

1 peeled potato, medium-
    size
1 small onion
1 egg
1 tablespoon flour

1 slice corned beef
seasoning
lard, dripping or oil for
    frying

METHOD

1 Grate the potato and onion into a bowl, using a
   coarse grater.
2 Add egg, flour, and corned beef cut small. Season.
3 Heat lard in a frying-pan, drop spoonfuls of the
   mixture into the pan and cook until golden and crisp
   on each side.
4 Drain on kitchen paper, and serve at once.

Spiced Grapefruit

Serves 1

Oven temperature: 400°F, gas mark 6 *or* cook under a
hot grill.

Cooking time: 8–10 minutes in oven, or about 5 minutes
under grill

INGREDIENTS

half a grapefruit

1 tablespoon brown sugar
(flat or heaped according
to taste)

a pinch of mixed spice

a little margarine (less than
half an oz.)

1 glacé cherry (optional)

METHOD

1 Loosen grapefruit from skin and cut into segments.
2 Sprinkle with brown sugar and mixed spice.
3 Dot with small knobs of margarine.
4 Cook in pre-heated oven 400°F, gas mark 6 for 8–10
   minutes or under a hot grill for about 5 minutes.
5 Serve hot with a cherry in the centre.

Steak and Kidney Crumble

This is easier to make than a steak and kidney pie.

Serves 2

Oven temperature: 325–350°F, gas mark 3–4

Cooking time: about 2 hours or a little longer

INGREDIENTS

half a pound of stewing steak

2–3 oz. kidney

seasoned flour – about 1
tablespoon flour mixed
with salt and pepper

2 medium onions

crumble mixture (4 oz.
flour, 2 oz. fat)

METHOD

1   Rinse kidney under running cold water. Trim surplus
    fat off steak. Cut up steak and kidney and coat with
    seasoned flour.

2   Pack into a small casserole with the sliced onion.
    Pour over about 1 teacup of water.

3   Put the lid on the casserole and bake at 325°F, gas
    mark 3 for 1 hour, 30 minutes.

4   Make a crumble with 4 oz. flour and 2 oz. fat – rub
    fat and flour together as for pastry until crumbly (or
    use 6 oz. ready-mix crumble, see page 147).

5   Put the crumble mixture on top of the steak and
    kidney. Bake in the oven with the lid off at 350°F,
    gas mark 4 until crumble is brown (at least 30–40
    minutes).

    This dish can be served hot or cold.

Steak Pan Pudding

Comment from Harlow Technical College classes:
'Students cut the cooking time of the meat by using
small tins of savoury mince in place of the stewing steak.
They cooked the vegetables first but omitted the onion.
No difficulties in preparation, all thought the one
saucepan idea a good one. They really enjoyed the
pudding.'

Serves 2

Cooking time: 1 hour, 30 minutes

You will need a small (2-pint) saucepan with a tightly fitting lid.

INGREDIENTS

8 oz. cubed stewing steak
1 small onion, peeled and
  chopped
2 carrots, peeled and sliced
1 small turnip (optional),
  peeled and sliced

1 oz. lard
1 tablespoon plain flour
half a pint of beef stock (use
  half a beef stock cube in
  half a pint of water)
salt and pepper

Pastry

3 oz. self-raising flour
3 rounded tablespoons
  packet shredded suet

pinch of salt
about 3 tablespoons water to
  mix

METHOD

1 Brown meat and lightly fry onion, carrot and turnip
   in melted lard.
2 Stir in the flour and cook for one minute.
3 Gradually add the stock, stirring all the time, bring
   to the boil and season.
4 Cover and simmer for one hour.
5 Meanwhile, mix together pastry ingredients to form
   a firm dough.
6 Roll or pat out pastry to a circle the size of the top
   of the pan.

7   Place pastry lid on contents of pan, replace saucepan lid and simmer for a further 30 minutes until pastry has risen and cooked.
8   Serve hot straight from the pan.

Steamed Roasting Chicken

Cooking time: one and a quarter hours approximately

Note. If using a frozen chicken, de-frost it thoroughly.

INGREDIENTS

1 small whole roasting
   chicken
1 small onion
1 small carrot

1 bay leaf
a thin strip of lemon rind
1 teaspoon salt
the chicken giblets

METHOD

1   Use a saucepan with a well-fitting lid just slightly larger than the washed and trussed chicken.
2   Pour into the saucepan about 1 inch of cold water, add the peeled onion and carrot, the bay leaf, lemon rind, salt and giblets. Last put in the chicken.
3   Bring to the boil, skim if necessary, put the lid on the pan and turn the heat down so that the water simmers gently. A small chicken weighing two and three quarter pounds or a little more will take about one hour, 15 minutes.

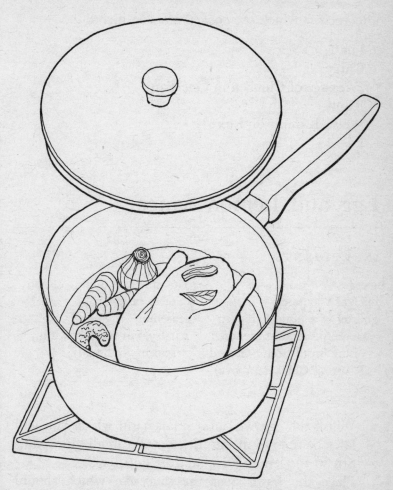

Note. This makes a very tender chicken for eating hot and the stock makes a good strong broth for chicken soup. Steamed roasting chicken is moist and succulent when eaten cold, far less dry than cold roasted chicken.

Our recipes which use cooked chicken include:

Pilaff
Curry
Fricassée of Chicken in One Pan
Risotto
Welsh Rarebit de Luxe

Egg and Lemon Sauce

INGREDIENTS

1 egg
juice of 1 lemon
quarter of a pint of chicken
    stock (preferably use some
    of the broth from Steamed
    Roasting Chicken, above)

1 teaspoon granulated sugar,
    or to taste
seasoning
parsley, cut roughly with
    scissors (optional)

METHOD

1 Whisk the egg well in a small basin which you will
   later be able to fit into the top of a small saucepan.
2 Stir in the lemon juice and the hot stock.
3 Place the basin over the saucepan which should
   contain an inch or two of near-boiling water. Keep
   the water in the pan very gently simmering. Stir the
   contents of the basin until the sauce thickens enough
   to coat the back of a wooden spoon.

4   Add sugar and seasoning to taste (this should be a
    sharp lemony sauce, so do not add too much sugar).
5   Stir in parsley and pour over the chicken, or serve
    in a separate sauce-boat.

Note. This is just as good cold with cold chicken – it
thickens a little on cooling.

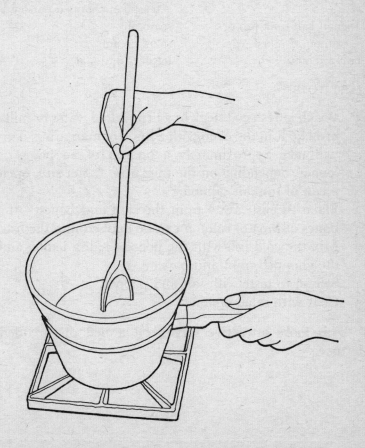

Summer Fish

Serves 1

INGREDIENTS

1 cod steak, cooked
or
1 small can tuna fish or
   salmon, drained
half a lemon

1 teaspoon chopped mint
1 teaspoon chopped parsley
seasoning
salad cream
lettuce (optional)

METHOD

1   Poach a fresh cod steak in a little salted water or milk,
    or bake it in the oven with a knob of margarine. This
    will take approximately a quarter of an hour, or
    longer, depending on the thickness. Easier still, open
    a can of tuna or salmon.
2   Flake the fish away from the skin and bones – the
    bones of tuna or salmon can be mashed into the fish.
3   Mix the cold fish with the juice of half a lemon and
    the chopped mint and parsley.
4   Season to taste with salt and pepper.
5   Coat with salad cream.

   This looks attractive served on a bed of shredded
lettuce.

Tomatoes – Quick Change

Serves 1

INGREDIENTS

1 slice white bread
2 large tomatoes, peeled* and halved
a good ounce of butter or margarine

seasoning
a sprinkle of demerara or granulated sugar
a dash of Worcestershire sauce

METHOD

1   Remove crusts then cut the bread into tiny cubes. Put bread cubes on one side.
2   Peel the tomatoes and fry in *plenty* of butter or margarine.
3   Season with salt, pepper, brown sugar and Worcestershire sauce.
4   Stir in the bread cubes and continue to fry until all the butter has been absorbed.

* Dip into a pan of boiling water for less than a minute, put under cold water to make them easy to handle: the skin slips off easily.

Tomato Sauce

INGREDIENTS

3 medium tomatoes or 1   1 medium cooking apple
  small can tomatoes   1–2 teaspoons vinegar
        —   brown sugar

METHOD

1 Cut up peeled tomatoes (see previous recipe), or use
   a small can of tomatoes, with peeled cored quartered
   cooking apple. Stew together till soft.
2 Add 1–2 teaspoons vinegar and sweeten to taste with
   brown sugar. Serve hot with fish or meat.

   Eat within one or two days, reheating before use.

Tripe and Onions

Serves 2

Cooking time: 1 hour, 20 minutes

INGREDIENTS

1 lb. tripe   salt and pepper
quarter of a pint of milk   half an ounce of butter
quarter of a pint of water   half an ounce of plain flour
1 large onion, sliced   (1 level tablespoon)

METHOD

1 Wash the tripe and cut in pieces.
2 Put in a pan with milk and water.
3 Add the onion.
4 Season and simmer for one hour.
5 Melt the butter, and add flour to make a roux (i.e. stir together over gentle heat for about 3 minutes until it forms a thick paste). Gradually add liquor from tripe, stirring well. Bring to the boil.
6 Add tripe to the sauce and simmer for a further 20 minutes.

Vegetable Omelette

For 2 ample servings

INGREDIENTS

a 4 oz. packet Birds Eye
  Mixed Vegetables
1 oz. margarine
2 oz. corned beef, chopped

2 standard eggs
2 tablespoons water
salt and pepper

METHOD

1 Cook the mixed vegetables according to the packet instructions.
2 Melt the margarine in a frying-pan and add the corned beef with the mixed vegetables.

3   Beat the eggs together with the water and seasoning, pour into the pan.
4   Cook the omelette gently, stirring with a fork until the egg just begins to set. Then lift the edges slightly to allow the unset mixture to run underneath the edge (use either the fork or a palette knife).
5   Place the pan under the grill to set the top, if necessary.
6   Serve the omelette flat and cut into 2 portions.

Welsh Rarebit

Serves 1

Cooking time: approximately 5 minutes

INGREDIENTS

knob of soft margarine
2 oz. Cheddar cheese, grated
1 tablespoon milk
3–4 drops Worcestershire
   sauce

a pinch of dry mustard
1 large slice, or 2 small slices
   bread, toasted and spread
   with margarine

METHOD

1   Mix all the ingredients together.
2   Spread over the toast.
3   Place under a hot grill until golden and serve immediately.

Welsh Rarebit de Luxe

1. *Buck Rarebit*

A poached egg placed on the grilled Welsh Rarebit.

2. *Bacon*

A grilled rasher or two placed on the grilled Welsh Rarebit.

3. *Tomato*

A sliced tomato placed on the toast, covered with the Welsh Rarebit and then grilled.

4. *Chicken or Ham*

Slices or pieces of cooked chicken or cooked ham placed on the toast, covered with the Welsh Rarebit and then grilled.

5. *Apple*

Thin slices of peeled crisp eating apple placed on the toast, covered with the Welsh Rarebit and then grilled.

Chapter 4
Favourites from the Cookery Classes

Apple Crumble

Serves 3–4 (good eaten cold next day with custard or top of the milk)

Oven temperature: 350–375°F, gas mark 4–5

Cooking time: 30–40 minutes

INGREDIENTS

for base:

either	*or*
three quarters of a pound of fresh cooking apples	a 15-oz. can apple pie filling
1 oz. sugar, or to taste	1 tablespoon sultanas (optional) with either the fresh or canned apples
2 tablespoons water	

for crumble:

3 oz. plain flour
one and a half ounces of margarine

} or four and a half ounces of crumble topping (page 147)

one and a half ounces of sugar
3 rounded tablespoons
  Marvel, or similar dried
  milk powder

for Chocolate Crumble add
  also: 1 rounded tablespoon
  sieved cocoa

METHOD

1 *Either* peel, quarter, core and slice apples, put with
   the water in a pie dish, sprinkle the 1 oz. sugar in
   centre of the layers of apple and stir in the sultanas
   if used

   or empty contents of can into pie dish and mix with
   the sultanas, if used.

2 Make the crumble by rubbing the margarine into
   the flour until the mixture resembles fine breadcrumbs. Stir in sugar, Marvel and, if making a
   chocolate crumble, the sieved cocoa also at this stage.

3 Sprinkle over the fruit.

4 Bake at 350–375°F, gas mark 4–5 for 30–40 minutes
   on middle shelf of oven.

Apple Parcel

As with all 'parcel' cooking, the taste of this is especially
good. The full flavour is sealed in.

Serves 1 or 2

Oven temperature: 350°F, gas mark 4

Cooking time: 25–30 minutes

You will need a piece of kitchen foil 12 inches square.

INGREDIENTS

a little butter
1 large cooking apple
a little lemon juice
1 rounded tablespoon
   sultanas

1 rounded dessertspoon soft
   brown sugar, or any
   available sugar

METHOD

1   Butter the inner surface of the square of kitchen foil.
2   Peel and slice the apple and pile up on the buttered
    foil.
3   Sprinkle with the lemon juice, and stir in the sultanas
    and sugar.
4   Screw up the ends of the foil centrally to make a
    parcel and bake in centre of oven at 350°F, gas mark
    4, for 25–30 minutes.
5   Turn out on to a fruit dish and serve with top of the
    milk.

Bakewell Tart

Serves 2–3

Oven temperature: 375°F, gas mark 5

Cooking time: 30 minutes

INGREDIENTS

Flan case

4–6 oz. shortcrust pastry –
   made by your usual
   method
or
two and a half oz. Stork
   or other margarine
1 tablespoon water
4 oz. plain flour (sieved)

Filling

1 tablespoon raspberry jam
one and a half oz. soft
   margarine
one and a half oz. castor
   sugar
1 large egg
1 oz. self-raising flour,
   sieved
1 oz. ground almonds
2–3 drops almond essence

METHOD

Flan case

1 *Either* roll out shortcrust pastry
   or place margarine, water and 2 tablespoons of the
   flour into a bowl. Cream with a fork until well
   mixed (half a minute). Stir in remaining flour to
   form a firm dough; knead until smooth.
2 Roll out and line a 6-inch flan ring or sandwich tin.

Filling

1 Spread jam in the bottom of the pastry case.
2 Place all the remaining ingredients into a bowl and
   beat well with a wooden spoon until mixed (2–3
   minutes).
3 Fill pastry case evenly with the mixture.

4 Bake on the middle shelf of a pre-heated moderate oven 375°F, gas mark 5 for approximately 30 minutes.
5 Dust with sieved icing sugar when cool.

Brown Bread, Quick Method

Oven temperature: 450°F, gas mark 8

Cooking time: 30 minutes

You will need a well-greased 1-lb. loaf tin and a large polythene bag (greased on the inside) into which the tin will fit loosely.

INGREDIENTS

4 oz. brown flour
4 oz. white flour
1 level teaspoon sugar
1 level teaspoon salt

1 teaspoon lard
1 teaspoon fresh yeast
quarter of a pint of water
1 tablespoon cracked wheat or crushed cornflakes

METHOD

1 Mix the flours and sift them with sugar and salt into a bowl.
2 Rub in fat.
3 Blend yeast in the water and add all at once.
4 Mix to a soft, scone-like dough (adding more flour if necessary) that leaves the bowl clean.

5 Turn out on to a lightly floured surface and knead the dough thoroughly (this may take 2 – 3 minutes) until it is smooth and elastic.

6 Shape the dough and put it in the greased tin, which should be about half-filled with it.

7 For a crusty finish, brush the top of the loaf with salted water and sprinkle with cracked wheat (if available) or crushed cornflakes.

8 Put to rise inside a large greased polythene bag (loosely tied) until the dough has doubled in size and springs back when lightly pressed with a floured finger. Rising times can be varied to suit your convenience:

     quick rise – half an hour in a warm place
     slower rise – one to one and a half hours on kitchen table
     overnight rise – up to 12 hours in a cold larder

9 Remove the bag. Bake the loaf on the middle shelf of a hot oven, 450°F, gas mark 8 for 30 minutes (when it is ready the loaf sounds hollow when tapped).

10 Turn out to cool on a wire rack.

If you cannot get fresh yeast, use 1 level teaspoon dried yeast instead and amend the above steps as follows:

1 Dissolve the sugar in the water (to get the best result water should be 110°F, or warm to the hand.

2 Sprinkle the dried yeast on top. Leave until frothy, about ten minutes.

3 Add to sieved flours, salt and rubbed-in lard.

4   Mix to fairly soft dough that leaves sides of bowl clean.

Continue with steps 5–10

For other recipes using yeast – write to the Flour Advisory Bureau whose address is given on page xiv.

Button Biscuits

Makes approximately 30 small biscuits (they keep well in a tin).

Oven temperature: 375°F, gas mark 5

Cooking time: 8–10 minutes

INGREDIENTS

3 oz. self-raising flour, sieved
pinch salt
3 oz. castor sugar
3 oz. Quick Quaker or similar rolled oats

3 oz. butter or margarine
1 level tablespoon golden syrup
half a level teaspoon bicarbonate of soda
1 tablespoon milk

METHOD

1   Mix together the flour, salt, sugar and oats.
2   Warm the butter or margarine and syrup together until the butter has melted. Stir into the dry ingredients.

3   Dissolve the bicarbonate of soda in the milk and add to the mixture. Mix well.

4   Form the mixture into *small* balls, the size of marbles. Place on a greased baking tray, well apart.
Bake in a pre-heated oven 375°F, gas mark 5, for 8–10 minutes until golden brown.

5   Cool for a few minutes on the baking tray, remove and cool on a wire rack.
Store in an airtight tin.

Note from Camden Cookery Classes: the addition of a teaspoon of ground ginger with the flour makes these into delicious gingernuts.

California Salad

Serves 2–3

INGREDIENTS

Equal quantities of:
natural yogurt
desiccated coconut

chopped mandarin oranges
chopped pineapple pieces
chopped marshmallows

To serve 2–3 use the equivalent of half a carton of each.

METHOD

1   Combine all the ingredients.
2   Chill, if possible, and serve.

Note from Cookery Classes: 'Generally popular, though people were a little reluctant to try it at first. The yogurt carton was used as a measure. Suggest the half carton yogurt left be used as a salad dressing.'

Cheese Savoury

In the following recipe, if you find whisking difficult, add whole egg to the crumb mixture.

Serves 1–2

Oven temperature: 400°F, gas mark 6

Cooking time: 25 minutes

INGREDIENTS

1 egg
1 oz. soft white breadcrumbs
   or 3 rounded tablespoons
   small cubes of white bread
a quarter of a pint of milk
half an oz. of margarine

salt and pepper
2 oz. grated cheese
1 tomato (optional) – cooked
   with Cheese Savoury or
   served raw as garnish

METHOD

1   Grease a pie dish ($\frac{3}{4}$–1-pint size) and add a layer of sliced tomato if liked.

2   If using cubes of bread, put to soak in the milk for 5 minutes. It is not necessary to soak the bread crumbs. Separate yolk from white of egg.

3 Place milk, with bread cubes or bread crumbs, and margarine in a pan and bring to the boil.
4 Cool a little, if necessary beat with a fork until smooth, then add seasonings, egg yolk and grated cheese.
5 Whisk white stiffly, fold through the mixture and pour at once into the greased pie dish.
6 Bake in a moderate oven 400°F, gas mark 6 until well risen, brown and crisp, about 25 minutes. Serve with raw tomato as a garnish if liked.

Note. This mixture can be cooked in a pastry flan case and served hot or cold with salad, or in small pastry cases and served as a hot savoury.

Chops in Foil

Most recipes using chops may be altered to cook the chops in a foil parcel, either singly or all together. They are served in the foil and can then be tipped onto the plate with their savoury juices. Chops wrapped in foil are deliciously tender and do not shrink nearly as much as grilled or fried chops.

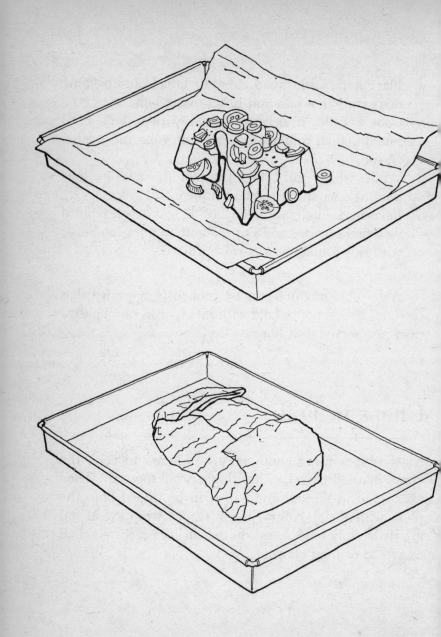

Italian Chops

Serves 2, or halve quantity for 1 person

Oven temperature: 425°F, gas mark 7

Cooking time: 40 minutes

You will need a piece of kitchen foil 18 inches square; for 1 chop foil needs to be only 12 inches square.

INGREDIENTS

1 small onion
2 ripe tomatoes
half a teaspoon dried mixed
   herbs
seasoning
1 teaspoon Worcestershire
   sauce

tip of a teaspoon sugar
2 lamb chops, trimmed of
   excess fat
small pat of butter
2 small scrubbed potatoes for
   baking in their jackets
   (optional)

METHOD

1 Dice onion, skin tomatoes (see page 113) and chop finely.
2 Mix onion, tomatoes, herbs, seasoning, sauce and sugar in a bowl.
3 Season the chops and spread with a little butter.
4 Place foil on baking tray and grease centre of foil with butter.
5 Put half the mixture on greased foil and lay buttered chops on this, cover with remaining mixture.

6   Fold up foil over chops, overlapping ends by two inches forming a parcel.
7   Bake for 40 minutes at 425°F, gas mark 7. Small baked potatoes in their jackets can be cooked at the same time.

Crumble Shortbread

This is easier than the normal kneading method.

Oven temperature: 325–350°F, gas mark 3–4

Cooking time: 30 minutes

INGREDIENTS

4 oz. plain flour
2 oz. cornflour, rice flour or
   custard powder*

4 oz. butter
2 oz. castor sugar, plus a
   little for sprinkling later

METHOD

1   Grease a sandwich tin.
2   Measure all ingredients into a bowl and rub in the butter until mixture is crumbly.
3   Put spoonfuls into the greased sandwich tin taking care to press down very gently. If pressed too hard the shortbread will be hard and tough.
4   Bake in a moderate oven (325–350°F, gas mark 3–4)

* *Note.* We have put custard powder as an alternative ingredient in this recipe as you may have it in the store-cupboard. But use cornflour or rice flour in preference – they give a better result in this recipe.

for about 30 minutes. The shortbread will be pale
golden and firm to the touch when cooked – but be
careful when touching it; it is hot.

5   Sprinkle a little more castor sugar over the top while
it is still hot, and leave to cool in the tin.
6   Divide the shortbread into sections while it is still
in the tin – though the correct way to serve is to
break off portions.

Date and Sultana Bread

Oven temperature: 325°F, gas mark 3

Cooking time: 1 hour

You will need a 1-lb. loaf tin, greased and lined on the
base with greased greaseproof paper

INGREDIENTS

one and a half tablespoons
    treacle
1 oz. butter
quarter of a pint of milk
6 oz. wholemeal (i.e. brown)
    flour
one and a half level teaspoons
    baking powder
quarter of a level teaspoon of
    salt
quarter of a level teaspoon
    of bicarbonate of soda

3 level tablespoons brown
    sugar
2 oz. dates, chopped or cut
    with scissors
2 tablespoons sultanas

} sieved together

METHOD

1   Warm the treacle, butter and milk together in a
    saucepan until the butter has melted.
2   Mix the remaining ingredients together in a mixing
    bowl.
3   Make a 'well' in the centre of the dry ingredients,
    add the liquid and mix to form a thick batter.
4   Pour into the base-lined and greased 1-lb. loaf tin and
    level the surface.
5   Bake for one hour at 325°F, gas mark 3 on the shelf
    just below the centre of the oven. Test with a skewer;
    it should come out clean, not sticky.

Note. Date and sultana bread keeps well; in an airtight
tin or wrapped in foil it will keep for about ten days. It
is delicious cut into thin slices and buttered.

For a *Date and Sultana Gingerbread*, add 1 heaped teaspoon ground ginger to the sieved ingredients.

Easter Biscuits

These are large, thin, cake-like biscuits and traditionally
should be given as a gift at Easter, in the form of 3 or 4
biscuits tied together with green or yellow ribbon.

12–14 biscuits

Oven temperature: 350°F, gas mark 4

Cooking time: 15 minutes

INGREDIENTS

6 oz. self-raising flour, sieved
2 oz. castor sugar
4 oz. butter

1 oz. currants
1 egg, separated
a sprinkle of castor sugar

METHOD

1 Mix flour and sugar.
2 Rub in the butter until the mixture resembles fine breadcrumbs.
3 Add currants.
4 Mix the yolk of the egg with 1 or 2 teaspoons of water, add to the mixture and work up a stiff dough.
5 Roll out fairly thinly (thickness of a 10p piece) and cut with a three to three-and-a-half inch fluted cutter.
6 Beat egg white until frothy and brush over the top of the biscuits, then sprinkle with castor sugar.
7 Place on a greased baking tray and bake in a pre-heated oven 350°F, gas mark 4 for 10–15 minutes.
8 Cool on a wire tray. Store in an airtight container.

Fish with Vegetables

Serves 2

Cooking time: approximately 20 minutes

INGREDIENTS

2 or 3 carrots, peeled and thinly sliced
1 small onion, peeled and thinly sliced

2 stalks celery, thinly sliced
1 oz. butter
half a lb. fish fillet (haddock, cod or other white fish)

2 tomatoes, peeled (see page   pinch of mixed herbs
  113) and chopped   1 tablespoon top of milk
1 tablespoon water   shake of pepper
half a bayleaf

METHOD

1   Cook the carrots, onion and celery gently in the
    butter until soft (this may take 10 minutes or longer
    with occasional stirring).
2   Cut fish into fairly large pieces and when the
    vegetables are cooked, add the fish to the pan and
    baste with the vegetables. Let this cook for a minute
    or two.
3   Add the peeled chopped tomatoes, a tablespoon of
    water and the bay leaf and herbs.
4   Cover the pan and cook for about 10 minutes or until
    the fish is done.
5   Remove fish to warm plates, add a tablespoon of the
    top of the milk and a shake of pepper to the vege-
    tables. Stir well, and then pour the vegetable mixture
    over the fish.

Note. I do not usually recommend a recipe which uses
only a stalk or so of celery because obviously one has to
buy a whole head of celery. However in this recipe the
celery gives such a delicious flavour that I felt it should
be included. A small head of celery suitable for cooking
can usually be bought quite cheaply. Use the rest of the
celery another day by braising it (see page 55) and
serving as a hot vegetable.

Fresh Fruit Salad

Yes, I know it is easier to open a can of fruit cocktail, but once you have tasted the refreshing flavour of this fresh fruit salad you will know why I have purposely suggested enough for several servings. It looks and tastes just as good next day. If you are visiting invalid or tired elderly friends, this is a treat you could prepare for them.

Serves 3–4

INGREDIENTS

3 level tablespoons granulated sugar
1 teacup water
juice of 1 lemon

fruit, e.g. 1 orange, 1 apple, 1 banana, 1 pear, other fresh fruit in season

METHOD

1   Bring the sugar and water to the boil, while stirring, then simmer without stirring it for approximately 5 minutes. Allow to cool.
2   Stir in the lemon juice.
3   Meanwhile peel and cut up the fruit and put it in a bowl. Pour the cold syrup over the fruit and leave for at least half an hour before serving.

Note. The 'ordinary' fruits were the most popular with the classes, with the addition of a few grapes, or soft fruits in season.

Fruit Flapjack

Serves 2 – just as nice eaten cold next day with top of the milk

Oven temperature: 400°F, gas mark 6

Cooking time: 30 minutes

INGREDIENTS

1 small can of plums, gooseberries, rhubarb or other favourite (not too sweet) fruit

1 oz. margarine

1 oz. brown sugar

1 tablespoon golden syrup

4 oz. Quick Quaker or similar rolled oats

METHOD

1   Drain the fruit of all but 2 or 3 tablespoons of the juice. (Remove the stones after cutting the plums in half.) Arrange the fruit in an ovenproof dish.
2   In a saucepan, melt the margarine with the brown sugar and syrup, stir in the oats and mix well together.
3   Place the oat mixture over the fruit.
4   Bake at 400°F, gas mark 6 for 30 minutes, until the topping begins to turn golden.

Note. Fresh fruit can be used instead, e.g. half a pound of fresh peeled, cored and roughly sliced cooking apples, sprinkled with 1 oz. granulated sugar and 2 or 3 tablespoons water.

Fruit Muesli

Use this recipe as a basic one. Add soft fruit or stewed fruit according to taste and season to give you plenty of variation in summer or winter. This is a nourishing recipe for brunch (breakfast-cum-lunch) or for tea or supper. By using Quick Quaker or similar oats there is no need to leave the oats soaking overnight – they are digestible eaten straight away.

Apples such as Cox's keep a good colour; some other varieties tend to brown on grating, but according to the classes testing this recipe 'the flavour is much enjoyed'.

Serves 1

INGREDIENTS

1 tablespoon Quick Quaker
  or similar oats
juice of half a lemon
top of the milk or single cream
a little sugar or honey
  (optional)
1 dessert apple
1 banana

other fruit, such as pears,
  grapes, stewed fruit or soft
  fruit in season
a few raisins or sultanas
a few crushed walnuts
  (optional)
glacé cherry for garnish
  (optional)

METHOD

1 In a bowl mix the oats, lemon juice and enough top of the milk or cream to make a thick pouring consistency. This will give a pleasantly sharp flavour to the finished dish. Sweeten with a little sugar or honey if you have a 'sweet tooth'.

2   Grate washed unpeeled apple into this mixture, stirring it well in to help prevent the apple from browning in the air.

3   Add other fruit to taste, peeling and cutting up where necessary. Garnish with a cherry if it needs extra colour.

Golden Cutlet and Egg Sauce

Serves 1–2

Cooking time: 5–10 minutes

INGREDIENTS

1 or 2 golden cutlets   1 egg
milk

METHOD

1   Cut off the fins and place fish in a pan (a frying-pan is usually best).

2   Almost cover with milk or milk and water.

3   Bring to the boil and simmer gently for 2 or 3 minutes, basting occasionally.

4   Remove from the pan and keep hot.

5   Break the egg into a basin and beat with a fork. Pour about quarter of a pint of milk from the pan on to the egg, stirring all the time.

6   Return to the pan and heat gently until thickened.

7   Pour over the fish and serve.

Grilled Herring – 1

Serves 1
Cooking time: 10 minutes

INGREDIENTS

half an oz. of butter
half a teaspoon vinegar
quarter of a teaspoon dry
  mustard
1 teaspoon grated onion

salt and pepper
1 herring, boned by the
  fishmonger
wedge of lemon
1 tomato, raw or grilled

METHOD

1 Soften butter and blend in the flavouring and seasoning ingredients.
2 Open the herring out flat, and spread this mixture
  over the flesh.
3 Grill gently, still opened-out flat, without turning the
  fish, for about 10 minutes.
4 Serve a wedge of lemon and a raw or grilled tomato
  with the herring.

Grilled Herring – 2

Serves 1
Cooking time: 15 minutes

INGREDIENTS

a tablespoon of your
  favourite chutney

1 herring, boned by the
  fishmonger

METHOD

1 Open the herring out flat, spread the flesh with chutney and fold in two again.
2 Season, and grill for about 7 minutes on one side.
3 Turn the fish, season and grill for a further 7 minutes until the fish is cooked and just beginning to brown.

Alternative Method for Grilled Herring – 2

The chutney herring can be baked in a foil parcel. Bake at 425°F, gas mark 7 for 15–20 minutes.

Lemon Sponge Pudding

Comment from Harlow Technical College Classes: 'The sponge rises, leaving a thick lemony sauce beneath. All liked this recipe very much and were very surprised how delicious the result was. Do use the soft easy-creaming margarine, it is so much easier to whisk than harder ones.'

Serves 2–3

Oven temperature: 350°F, gas mark 4

Cooking time: 20–30 minutes

You will need a medium-sized pie dish (of about three quarters of a pint capacity)

INGREDIENTS

juice and rind of half a lemon
1 oz. Blue Band or similar soft, easy-creaming margarine
2 oz. castor sugar
1 egg, separated
1 oz. self-raising flour, sieved
quarter of a pint (8 tablespoons) water

METHOD

1   Weigh and prepare all ingredients, placing all but the egg white in a mixing bowl.
2   Whisk egg white fairly stiffly in another bowl.
3   Whisk all ingredients (except egg white) in the mixing bowl until smooth (2–3 minutes).
4   Fold in the beaten egg white carefully, using a metal spoon. Pour into a greased three-quarter-pint pie dish.
5   Bake in pre-heated moderate oven, 350°F, gas mark 4 on middle shelf for 20–30 minutes.
6   Serve warm, sprinkled with castor sugar.

Lentil Cream Soup

Serves 2–3

Cooking time: approximately 1 hour, 15 minutes

INGREDIENTS

2 oz. lentils
1 small carrot
1 small onion
a small piece of celery
    (optional)
a small piece of turnip
half an oz. of butter

half a pint of milk
half a pint of stock (can be made from half a stock cube with water)
seasoning
half a tablespoon chopped parsley

METHOD

1   Wash and drain lentils.
2   Wash, peel and chop vegetables and fry gently in butter for 10 minutes.

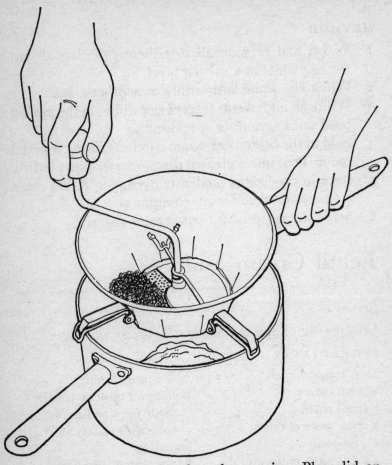

3 Add lentils, milk, stock and seasoning. Place lid on saucepan and simmer gently for 45 minutes.

4 Rub soup through a sieve (this is particularly easy if you have a fine Mouli-légumes sieve or a liquidizer).

5 Reheat slowly.

6 Decorate with chopped parsley.

Liver Fricassée

Serves 1

INGREDIENTS

2 or 3 thin slices of lamb's or pig's liver

margarine

For sauce

half an oz. of soft margarine
half an oz. of plain flour
quarter of a pint of milk

seasoning
pinch mixed herbs
a little lemon juice

Garnish

chopped parsley, a wedge of lemon

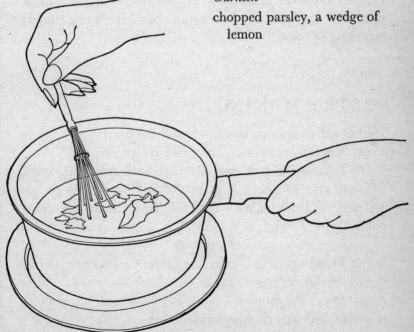

METHOD

1   Fry liver gently in the margarine until lightly cooked.
2   To make the sauce: put all the ingredients in a small
    saucepan and whisk until the sauce boils. Stir for 2–3
    minutes until cooked.
3   Cut liver into bite-size pieces, return them to the pan
    in which they were fried, add the sauce to this pan
    and heat well through.
4   Sprinkle with roughly chopped parsley, serve with a
    wedge of lemon.

Note. Optional additions to this dish – a few mushrooms cooked with the liver; some peas, fresh or canned;
croûtons of toast.

PASTRY MAKING

Whenever recipes in this book call for pastry,

(a) Keep to your own favourite recipe; *or*

(b) Follow the fork-mix method with soft margarine
that we give in detail (e.g. in the Bakewell Tart recipe
on page 121). You may find this easier than the usual
rubbing-in method; *or*

(c) Buy ready-made pastry; *or*

(d) Make up pastry from the Short Crust Pastry Mix,
details given on page 146; *or*

(e) Make the following Milk Pastry, which has proved
popular with the cookery classes.

Milk Pastry

Comment from Coventry Technical College Retirement Cookery Class: 'Milk Pastry was used for both sweet and savoury pies. It was soft to handle and short; it reheated very well without drying out or becoming hard. It browned quickly so needed watching and we turned the oven down to prevent over-cooking. Milk pastry is a little thicker than one made with plain flour but the students were well pleased with it.'

INGREDIENTS

8 oz. self-raising flour, sieved
2 oz. cooking fat or lard
2 oz. butter or margarine

1 heaped tablespoon Marvel or similar dried milk, mixed to a liquid with 3 tablespoons cold milk

METHOD

1 Rub the fats into the sifted flour until it resembles fine breadcrumbs.
2 Sprinkle the milk mixture over the top and mix well, using a knife to prevent over-handling.
3 Gather together in a ball and knead very lightly on a floured surface.
4 Roll out and use as required. Bake at 400°F, gas mark 6.

Short Crust Pastry Mix

Uses: Sweet or savoury pies, tarts, flans, tartlets, crumble topping

INGREDIENTS

8 oz. plain flour   2 oz. margarine
a pinch of salt   2 oz. lard

Note: The above is half fat to flour. If you make a lot of pastry dishes you may like to store a pastry mix made from 1 lb. of flour, 4 oz. margarine and 4 oz. of lard.

METHOD

1   Sift together flour and salt into a mixing bowl.
2   Rub in fats until mixture resembles fine breadcrumbs.
3   Store in a tightly closed polythene bag or jar in refrigerator for up to 3 months, or in a cool dark place below 60°F for 2–3 weeks. Take out of refrigerator 30 minutes before use.

To make up short crust pastry

1   For a recipe calling for '4 oz. short crust pastry' measure out 6 oz. of crumble (i.e. 4 oz. flour which is already mixed with 2 oz. fat); similarly if you need '6 oz. short crust pastry' you would need 9 oz. of crumble (i.e. 6 oz. flour which is mixed with half its weight, 3 oz., of fat).
2   To every 6 oz. crumble sprinkle in 1 tablespoon of cold water and mix to a stiff dough with a knife.

3 Turn on to a lightly floured board and knead lightly until smooth.
4 Roll out to required shape and thickness of pastry. (Bake small tarts and thin pastry cases at 400°F, gas mark 6 for 10–15 minutes; bake larger pastry cases in a fairly hot oven 425°F, gas mark 7 for 20–25 minutes.)

To make a crumble topping (see Apple Crumble, page 118) Omit water and add sugar to the dry mix – to 6 oz. crumble add 2 oz. demerara sugar. Or, instead of sugar, add a little seasoning or a few herbs for a savoury mix (see Steak and Kidney Crumble, page 105).

Peppermint Creams

20–25 peppermint creams

INGREDIENTS

1 oz. margarine
1 tablespoon milk
a few drops of peppermint
  essence

a few drops of green colouring
half a lb. icing sugar, sieved
icing sugar for kneading and
  rolling

METHOD

1 Melt together the margarine, milk, peppermint essence and green colouring and allow to cool slightly. (With a medium-strength peppermint essence you may need 8–10 drops.)

2   Add the sieved icing sugar and mix well with a
     wooden spoon to form a stiff paste.
3   Sieve a little extra icing sugar onto the table and
     knead the paste well.
4   *Either* roll out quarter of an inch thick, and cut into
       rounds using a 1-inch cutter;
     or roll teaspoons of the mixture into small balls and
       flatten with a fork.
5   Allow to dry out at room temperature for an hour
     or more before storing.

Pineapple Meringue Pudding

Serves 2

Oven temperature: 300°F, gas mark 2

Cooking time: 15–20 minutes

INGREDIENTS

1 level tablespoon cornflour
1 can pineapple chunks
  (about 7½ oz.)
6 tablespoons milk
half an oz. of margarine

1 level tablespoon sugar
1 egg yolk (standard size)
  beaten
grated plain chocolate
  (optional)

Meringue Topping

1 egg white (standard size)

one and a half oz. of castor
  sugar

METHOD

1 Blend the cornflour with 2 tablespoons of pineapple juice from can. Place in a small saucepan with milk and margarine. Bring to the boil, stirring all the time, and cook for 2–3 minutes.

2 Remove from the heat and stir in the sugar and egg yolk.

3 Arrange pineapple in a greased three-quarter-pint pie dish, and pour cornflour mixture on top. (If you like, at this stage, grate a little plain chocolate over the top of the pudding.)

4 For the meringue topping, whisk egg white stiffly and add half the sugar. Whisk again until stiff and fold in remaining sugar. Pile on top of the pudding and cover surface completely.

5 Bake in a pre-heated oven 300°F, gas mark 2 for 15–20 minutes.

6 Serve hot or cold.

Pineapple Upside-down Pudding

Serves 3–4

Oven temperature: 325°F, gas mark 3

Cooking time: 25–35 minutes

You will need a 6-inch sandwich tin.

INGREDIENTS

Topping

half an oz. of margarine
1 level tablespoon soft   } melted together
   brown sugar
3 rings pineapple
2 glacé cherries

Pudding

2 oz. Stork or similar
   soft margarine
2 oz. castor sugar
1 egg, large and unbeaten
2 oz. self-raising flour
half a level teaspoon   } sieved together
   baking powder

METHOD

1 Grease and bottom line a 6-inch sandwich tin.
   (Do not be confused when we tell you to put the
   topping on the bottom of the tin; this is an upside-
   down pudding, so read on.)
2 Spread topping ingredients over the bottom and
   arrange pineapple and cherries attractively.
3 Place all pudding ingredients together in a bowl and
   beat with a wooden spoon until well mixed (2–3
   minutes).

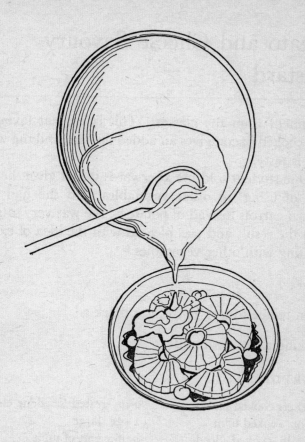

4 Spread carefully over the pineapple.
   Bake in a pre-heated warm oven 325°F, gas mark 3
   on middle shelf for 25–35 minutes.
5 Turn out carefully on to a serving dish.

Note. If you have any pineapple rings left over, use
for Pineapple Salad, see page 30.

Potato and Cheese Savoury Custard

Comment from the classes: 'This is a great favourite. The cooked bacon gives an added flavour, and the whole dish is tasty.

'One student told me afterwards it had given her the idea of using up other vegetables, and she had used cooked carrots instead of potatoes; she was very satisfied with the result and was pleased with the idea of experimenting with other vegetables.'

Serves 2

Oven temperature: 325°F, gas mark 3

Cooking time: 40 minutes

INGREDIENTS

2 rashers cooked bacon, or
   1 oz. cooked ham
half a lb. cooked sliced
   potato

2 oz. grated Cheddar cheese
1 egg, large
half a pint of milk
salt and pepper

METHOD

1 Grease an ovenproof dish with margarine or butter.
2 Chop the bacon or ham.
3 Place in the dish in layers: potato, cheese, bacon, potato, cheese.

4   Beat the egg, add the milk and seasoning, pour over the layers in the dish.
5   Bake, uncovered, at 325°F, gas mark 3 for 40 minutes or until the custard is set.

Potato and Milk Soup

Serves 2

Cooking time: 20–30 minutes

INGREDIENTS

half a pint of milk
1 medium raw potato
half a small onion (or 1
   teaspoon dried onion)

salt and pepper
2 tablespoons grated cheese
chopped parsley (optional)

METHOD

1   Put the milk into a saucepan.
2   Peel the potato and fresh onion and grate into the milk (or add dried onion to avoid grating fresh onion).
3   Simmer gently until tender, 20–30 minutes.
4   Add seasoning to taste.
5   Serve sprinkled with grated cheese and parsley.

Alternative suggestions:

Grate extra vegetables to give additional flavour and to make a vegetable soup.

Sieve the cooked soup for a smoother texture.

SAUCER PIES

These individual pies do not need a special tin; they can be baked on old china saucers – the saucer will not break in the heat of the oven. Try savoury egg and bacon, or sweet fruit or jam saucer pies.

Egg and Bacon Saucer Pies

Serves 2

Oven temperature and cooking time: 400°F, gas mark 6 for 15 minutes, reduce to 325°F, gas mark 3 for the next 10–15 minutes

INGREDIENTS

Pastry

two and a half oz. Stork, or
  similar soft margarine

1 tablespoon water
4 oz. plain flour, sieved

Filling

4 rashers streaky bacon,
  chopped and fried in
  half an oz. of margarine
  (a small knob)
2 standard eggs, beaten

2 tablespoons milk
a pinch of pepper
a pinch of mixed herbs
  (optional)
milk to glaze

METHOD

To make pastry

1 Place margarine, water and 2 tablespoons flour in bowl and cream together with fork until well mixed (half a minute).

2 Stir in remaining flour to form a firm dough.

3 Knead lightly on a floured board. Divide in half.
   Roll out thinly to cut two rounds from each half, slightly larger than the saucer.
   Line the two saucers with the first two rounds of pastry and prick to prevent rising.

To make filling and finish pies

4 Combine all ingredients and pour into the two saucers.

5 With a little water damp round the edges of the pastry in the saucers. Cover tops of saucers with the third and fourth rounds and press on firmly.
   Brush with milk.

6 Place on baking sheet and bake in pre-heated hot oven, 400°F, gas mark 6, for 15 minutes, then reduce heat to 325°F, gas mark 3 for 10–15 minutes.

Note. If you prefer, this can be baked on a 6-inch pie plate or sandwich tin as one pie sufficient for 2–3 servings. For this one larger pie, bake at 400°F, gas mark 6 for 25 minutes then reduce heat to 325°F, gas mark 3 for the next 10–15 minutes.

For Sweet Saucer Pies

Make in the same way, but put in a filling of mincemeat and chopped apple, or canned gooseberries, plums or rhubarb. *Or* make uncovered pies, filled with jam or mincemeat. Uncovered pies cook in 15 minutes altogether.

SCONES

Most general cookery books give recipes for scones made by the rubbing-in method, with the fat rubbed into the flour. This gives perfectly good results, but if you use one of the new soft margarines you may find this modern all-in-one method easier. Also, made by this method, including an egg, they keep extra well until the next day in an airtight tin. If you use a harder fat, keep to the usual rubbing-in method.

Plain Scones

Makes 6–8 scones

Oven temperature: 425°F, gas mark 7

Cooking time: 12–15 minutes

INGREDIENTS

4 oz. self-raising flour
half a level teaspoon   } sieved together
   baking powder
a pinch of salt
1 oz. Stork or similar   1–2 tablespoons milk
   soft margarine   1 standard egg (unbeaten)
1 level tablespoon castor   milk to glaze (optional)
   sugar

Note. If you wish to double the quantities to make twice as many scones, still keep to one egg only whilst doubling the other ingredients.

METHOD

1 Place all ingredients in a mixing bowl and mix well together with a wooden spoon to form the scone dough.
2 Turn out onto a lightly floured board and knead lightly.
3 *Either* roll out to half-inch thickness and, using a 2-inch cutter, cut into rounds
   or press into a round about half-an-inch thick. With the blunt side of a knife mark deeply into 6–8 wedge shapes, but do not cut right through.
4 Place scones or round on a baking sheet and brush the top with milk to glaze if you wish.
   Bake in pre-heated oven 425°F, gas mark 7 for 12–15 minutes.

5   Cool on a wire tray.
    Whilst still warm, cut the round through the mark-
    ings to make 6–8 wedge-shaped scones.

Fruit Scones

To the ingredients for plain scones
    add 2 oz. currants or sultanas.

METHOD

As above.

Cheese Scones

To the ingredients for plain scones add
a pinch of dry mustard
one and a half oz. medium to full-flavoured Cheddar
cheese, grated

omit the 1 tablespoon castor sugar.

METHOD

As above.

*

Speedy Mix Chocolate Cake

Comment from Sheffield cookery classes: 'This was thought to be a very good recipe. They were surprised that an eggless cake recipe could turn out so well.'

Oven temperature: 350°F, gas mark 4

Cooking time: 20–25 minutes

You will need two 6-inch sandwich tins, or one 8-inch sandwich tin.

INGREDIENTS

4 oz. plain flour
4 oz. castor sugar
2 rounded tablespoons cocoa
large pinch bicarbonate of soda
half a level teaspoon baking powder
quarter of a level teaspoon salt
4 fluid oz. milk
half a teaspoon vinegar
2 fluid oz. corn oil
few drops vanilla essence

METHOD

1 Grease and line the base of two 6-inch sandwich tins or one 8-inch sandwich tin with greased greaseproof paper or ungreased Bakewell non-stick paper.

2 Sieve all the dry ingredients together into a mixing bowl.

3 Whisk together the milk, vinegar, corn oil and vanilla essence with a fork, and add to the dry ingredients. Beat well with a wooden spoon to form a smooth slack mixture. Turn into prepared tins.

4 Bake in a moderate oven 350°F, gas mark 4 for about 20 minutes (8-inch tin requires 25 minutes). Cake should be firm to the touch and have just shrunk away from the side of the tin.

5 Cool on a cake tray, remove paper carefully.

6 To decorate the single 8-inch cake, sieve a little icing sugar over the top. To sandwich together the

two 6-inch cakes, use One-stage Icing or Filling (page 163) preferably making the chocolate or coffee variation.

Sweet and Sour Spare-ribs of Lamb

Serves 4. 2 servings hot one day, 2 servings cold the next day

Oven temperature: 325°F, gas mark 3, reduce later to 300°F, gas mark 2

Cooking time: 1 hour, 10 minutes or a little longer

INGREDIENTS

a whole unboned breast of lamb, meaty and of good quality	1 tablespoon golden syrup
	1 dessertspoon vinegar (malt or wine vinegar)
salt and pepper	

METHOD

1   Season the lamb and roast for 40 minutes at 325°F, gas mark 3.
2   Remove to a dish so that you can pour off the fat from the tin.
3   Turn down oven to 300°F, gas mark 2.
4   Take two tablespoons of the fat poured off from the tin and put it in a saucepan with the golden syrup and vinegar. Bring to boil.

5   Return the lamb to the tin and pour over the sauce
    from the pan.
6   Return to the oven for half an hour or more, basting
    and turning.

   Note. A small scrubbed potato about 4-oz. size can be
baked in its jacket at the same time.
   This sweet and sour recipe is also suitable for ribs of
pork.

Victoria Sponge Cake

Oven temperature: 325°F, gas mark 3

Cooking time: 25–35 minutes

You will need a 7-inch sandwich tin, greased and lined
on the base with greased greaseproof paper.

INGREDIENTS

2 oz. Stork or similar
   soft margarine
2 oz. castor sugar
1 large egg
2 oz. self-raising flour
half a level teaspoon baking   } sieved together
   powder

METHOD

1   Place all ingredients in a mixing bowl, beat with a
    wooden spoon until smooth (2–3 minutes).

2   Place in a 7-inch sandwich tin, greased and base-lined.
3   Bake on a middle shelf of the pre-heated oven, 325°F, gas mark 3 for 25–35 minutes.
4   Cool on a wire tray.

Note. To make a moist 7-inch Chocolate Victoria Sponge, replace 1 tablespoon flour with a tablespoon cocoa; and add 1 good teaspoon of black treacle.

'One-stage' Icing or Filling

INGREDIENTS

one and a half oz. of soft margarine

4 oz. icing sugar, sieved

1 dessertspoon milk or fruit juice

METHOD

Place all ingredients in mixing bowl and beat until well mixed (2–3 minutes).

Variations

Chocolate: blend 1 dessertspoon cocoa with 1 tablespoon hot water, cool and add to basic recipe instead of the milk.

Orange or lemon: use fruit juice instead of milk. Add colouring.

Coffee: replace 1 dessertspoon milk by 1 dessertspoon Camp Coffee Essence.

Chapter 5
Store-cupboard Cookery

Bad weather or temporary illness can keep even the most enthusiastic shoppers indoors. Many other men and women are permanently housebound and for them shopping is often a matter of relying on others to bring in their food.

Under these conditions it is all too easy to find yourself living on dull and boring snacks and limiting your enjoyment of meal times.

This chapter has been written to help you with your difficulties. As well as the usual background stocks of milk and eggs, flour, sugar, tea and other dried goods, if you have the following items in stock you will be able to make, without need of shopping, all the recipes in this chapter. Look through the other chapters too: the goods listed below will enable you to cook many of the other recipes from your stores. This is a comprehensive list, but if you have a limited income or limited storage space, you can choose from this check-list the items of greatest value to you.

Beverages

canned orange juice,
    cocoa
condensed milk
lime cordial
Marvel or similar
    skimmed milk powder
pure lemon juice
rose-hip syrup
soups, including
    condensed and dried
vitamin C blackcurrant
    drink

Cereals

breakfast cereals
canned milk puddings
cornflour
ground rice
macaroni
rice
rolled oats
spaghetti

Fats

butter, margarine,
    including easy-
    creaming margarine,
    cooking fat
cooking oil, shredded suet

Fish (canned)

herring roes
kippers
sardines
tuna or salmon

Flavourings

mixed herbs and other
    favourite herbs
mixed spice, paprika and
    other favourite spices
pickles and chutneys
tomato puree and ketchup
Worcestershire sauce

Fruit and Vegetables

canned fruits, including
    baby-food cans
canned vegetables,
    including canned
    tomatoes
instant potato and other
    dried vegetables,
    including dried onions

Meat (*canned*)

corned beef
luncheon meat
minced meat
stewing steak

Other Groceries

biscuits
black treacle
dried fruits, including
    glacé cherries
desiccated coconut
golden syrup

Other Groceries – contd

jellies
marmalade and jam
packet sauces
plain chocolate bar
stock cubes, yeast extract
    and meat extract
sugars (including brown
    and icing)

Useful Item

short crust pastry mix,
    see page 146

Baked Custard

Serves 2

The addition of the milk powder gives extra nourishment and creaminess.

Oven temperature: 300°F, gas mark 2

Cooking time: 1 hour

INGREDIENTS

1 standard egg
one and a half level
    tablespoons Marvel or
    similar skimmed milk
    powder

1 level tablespoon granulated
    sugar
half a pint of milk
grated nutmeg (optional)

METHOD

1   Beat egg, skimmed milk powder and sugar together.
2   Heat milk, do not boil, and pour onto egg mixture.
    Strain into an ovenproof dish. Sprinkle with a little
    nutmeg to taste.
3   Bake in a slow oven 300°F, gas mark 2, until the
    custard is set, about 1 hour.

Cherub Dumplings

Serves 2

Cooking time: 8–10 minutes

INGREDIENTS

2 oz. self-raising flour
2 rounded tablespoons packet
   shredded suet
1 level tablespoon castor
   sugar

1 level tablespoon desiccated
   coconut
4 glacé cherries, chopped
half a pint of milk

METHOD

1   Mix together flour, suet, sugar, coconut and cherries
    with a little of the measured milk to make a firm
    dough.
2   Shape mixture into four balls.
3   Simmer dumplings gently in remaining milk for
    8–10 minutes, with the lid on the pan.
4   Serve hot with milk liquor poured over.

Chocolate Fudge Bars

Quantity: 10

No baking: leave to harden in 7-inch-square shallow
  cake tin or similar sized dish

INGREDIENTS

4 oz. margarine

4 oz. castor sugar

2 level tablespoons cocoa

3 level tablespoons Marvel
  milk, or similar skimmed
  milk powder

1 egg, beaten

4 oz. sultanas

half a lb. of biscuits, broken
  into tiny pieces

a little icing sugar

METHOD

1 Melt the margarine and sugar in a pan, stir in cocoa,
   Marvel and the lightly beaten egg.
2 Remove from heat, mix in sultanas and biscuits.
3 Place mixture into the tin, pressing it down well and
   levelling off the surface. Mark the top with a fork.
4 Leave to harden. Dust with sifted icing sugar and cut
   into ten pieces.

  These are particularly popular if you are teaching
children how to cook – or to give them if they come to
tea.

Chocolate Mousse

Serves 1
(quantities can be multiplied for more servings)

INGREDIENTS

1 oz. plain chocolate   1 egg, separated
1 teaspoon milk or water

METHOD

1 Melt the chocolate slowly with the milk or water in a basin over pan of hot (not boiling) water, stirring to blend.
2 Remove from the heat and beat in the egg yolk.
3 Whisk egg white until stiff and carefully fold into chocolate mixture.
4 Pour into a small dish and leave to cool.

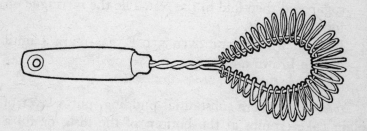

Fruit Meringue

Serves 1 or 2

Oven temperature: 350°F, gas mark 4

Cooking time: approximately 15 minutes

INGREDIENTS

1 can fruit baby food (e.g.
  raspberry, apple and rose-
  hip; junior peaches;
  orange delight; apple)

1 large egg
a little lemon juice
2 oz. castor sugar

METHOD

1 Turn the fruit out of the tin into a small pie dish or casserole.
2 Beat in the egg yolk and add a little lemon juice if necessary to sharpen the flavour.
3 Whisk the egg white until very stiff, whisk in half the sugar and then fold in the rest. Pile the meringue on top of the fruit.
4 Bake in a moderate oven 350°F, gas mark 4 until golden brown and crisp.

Note. For a more substantial pudding, put a layer of plain cake crumbs at the bottom of the dish, or fill a cooked, short crust pastry flan with the fruit meringue to make a fruit meringue pie.

Goulash ✗

Serves 2, or one serving one day and, thoroughly re-heated, a second serving next day.

Cooking time: 15 minutes

INGREDIENTS

a knob of margarine or
   dripping
1 level tablespoon plain flour
1 tablespoon dried onion
1 can stewed steak (7½ oz.)
1 tablespoon tomato puree
1 level teaspoon paprika

a scant quarter pint stock
   (quarter of a beef stock
   cube dissolved in quarter
   of a pint of water)
seasoning
mashed potato or boiled rice

METHOD

1   Melt fat in a saucepan.
2   Add flour, onion, stewed steak, tomato puree and paprika and cook for 2–3 minutes, stirring continuously.
3   Add stock, season to taste, simmer gently with the lid on the pan for 10–12 minutes.
4   Serve on a bed of mashed potato, or of plain boiled rice.

Ham and Vegetable Rice

Serves 2

Cooking time approximately 25–30 minutes

INGREDIENTS

4 oz. cooked ham or luncheon meat, diced*

2 tablespoons cooked peas, or 5-oz. can garden peas

2 oz. chopped onion, or 1 heaped teaspoon dried onion

1 can peeled tomatoes (8 oz.) with the juice

salt and pepper to taste

quarter of a pint of stock

2 oz. uncooked long-grain rice

METHOD

1   Combine all ingredients except rice in a saucepan and bring to the boil. Simmer for 10 minutes.

2   Stir in the rice. Bring back to the boil and stir once, lower the heat and simmer. Cover the pan and cook for about 15 minutes, or until the rice is soft and the liquid is absorbed.

* Cheaper alternative, suggested by Bedale Agricultural Centre Retirement Class: 'Use bacon pieces, first fried then added to ingredients, in place of ham or luncheon meat.' This, of course, takes it out of the 'store-cupboard cookery' chapter, but is well worth trying.

Herring Roes on Toast

Serves 1

INGREDIENTS

4 oz. herring roes (fresh or –
for a storecupboard
recipe – canned roes)
approximately 1 level
tablespoon plain flour

salt and pepper
1 oz. butter, or margarine
1 slice of bread
butter and Marmite for
spreading

METHOD

1 Season flour with salt and pepper and toss the roes
in it (easily done if you shake them all together in a
clean paper bag).
2 Melt butter in a small frying–pan, and fry roes for
4–5 minutes, turning them in the pan until they are
lightly browned.
3 Toast the bread. Spread with butter and Marmite.
4 Place the roes on the Marmite toast, and pour any
butter still in the pan, over them.
5 Serve piping hot.

Meat Roly-Poly

Serves 4: two servings hot one day; two servings cold
the next day.

Oven temperature: 375°F, gas mark 5

Cooking time: 55 minutes

INGREDIENTS

Pastry	*Filling*
4 oz. self-raising flour	8 oz. can minced steak and
4 rounded tablespoons	onion
shredded suet	half a teaspoon mixed herbs
half a teaspoon salt	2 teaspoons fresh or dried
cold water for mixing	parsley

METHOD

1   Sift flour and salt together into a bowl, add suet, mix with cold water to a stiff consistency.
2   Roll into an oblong.
3   Mix together minced steak, mixed herbs and parsley.
4   Spread this mixture over the pastry, damp the edges with water and roll up lengthways, pressing the edges lightly to seal. Place on a greased baking tray.
5   Cook in the centre of the pre-heated oven for 55 minutes at 375°F, gas mark 5.

Oat Corned Beefburgers

Serves 2–3

Cooking time: approximately 10 minutes

INGREDIENTS

6 oz. corned beef	2 teaspoons tomato ketchup
1 oz. rolled oats	1 teaspoon Worcestershire
1 small onion (finely	sauce
chopped) or 1 tablespoon	salt and pepper
dried onion flakes	1 standard egg, beaten

For coating and frying

flour   fat

METHOD

1   Crumble the corned beef into a basin and add the remainder of the ingredients, except the egg.
2   Mash with a fork. Add the beaten egg.
3   Divide the mixture into 4 or 6 portions, shape into flat round cakes.
4   Coat with flour, pressed firmly with a knife.
5   Heat fat in the frying-pan and fry 'burgers' gently for 4–5 minutes on each side.

Raspberry Honeycomb

Serves 2–3

INGREDIENTS

1 small can raspberries   1 egg, separated
half a packet raspberry jelly

METHOD

1   Strain the fruit and set aside.
2   To the juice add sufficient water to make 8 oz. (If you have no fluid ounces marked on a measure, reckon 8 oz. to equal 12 tablespoons.) Heat the liquid and dissolve the jelly in it. Allow to cool approximately 3 minutes.
3   Beat the egg yolk into the slightly cooled liquid. Add the fruit.

4   Whisk the egg white until fairly stiff, cut and fold into the mixture with a metal spoon.

5   Pour into serving dish, or individual glasses, and leave to set. The mixture will separate with a fruit jelly underneath and a frothy pink layer on top.

Savoury Soufflé

This is more expensive than the simple one-stage cheese soufflé, but may be a more convenient alternative, if you already have a packet of sauce-mix, or a small can of condensed soup in your cupboard.

Serves 2

Note. For a single serving make up half the recipe and cook in a 3-inch-diameter soufflé dish.

Oven temperature: 375°F, gas mark 5

Cooking time: approximately 25 minutes (15–20 minutes for single serving)

INGREDIENTS

either

one packet sauce-mix (e.g. cheese flavour)
and
quarter of a pint of milk (8 tablespoons)

or

a 6 oz. can of condensed soup (e.g. mushroom, chicken or celery)

2 eggs, separated

METHOD

1 Grease a 5-inch-diameter ovenproof dish, preferably a soufflé dish.

2 *If using sauce-mix*
In a medium-sized saucepan (*and using only quarter pint milk*) make up the sauce by the method given on the packet. Remove this thick sauce from the heat and allow to cool for a minute or two.
If using condensed soup
In a medium-sized saucepan, stir the undiluted contents of the can until smooth and hot, then remove this thick 'sauce' from the heat and allow to cool for a minute or two.

3 Stir in the egg yolks.

4 Whisk the egg whites stiffly, then with a large metal spoon, gently cut and fold the egg whites into the contents of the saucepan.

5   Pour into the dish and bake in a fairly hot oven,
    375°F, gas mark 5 for approximately 25 minutes
    (approximately 15–20 minutes for single serving) till
    well risen and golden.
6   Serve at once.

Soufflé Ground Rice

Serves 2

INGREDIENTS

1 tablespoon ground rice   half a pint of milk
1 tablespoon sugar   1 egg, separated
1 tablespoon cocoa (optional)

METHOD

1   Place ground rice and sugar in basin and mix with a
    little milk to a paste.*
2   Boil the rest of the milk and pour over the ground
    rice, stirring all the time.
3   Return to the pan and, stirring constantly, bring to
    the boil. Simmer for 5 minutes, stirring frequently.
4   Separate egg and add yolk to pan, stirring in rapidly
    off the heat.
5   Beat the egg white until stiff, and fold into the
    mixture in the pan very carefully.

   * To vary flavour, 1 tablespoon cocoa may be added to the
ground rice and sugar when mixing to a paste.

This pudding may be served straight from the pan into individual dishes, or placed in a pie dish and kept hot in the oven.

It can be eaten hot or cold.

If plain try it served with vitamin C blackcurrant syrup or rose-hip syrup.

Soup Scramble

Serves 2

For one person use 2 standard eggs to the one small can of soup.

Cooking time: 3 or 4 minutes

INGREDIENTS

3 eggs
1 small 6-oz. can condensed
   soup (celery, asparagus,
   mushroom or chicken are
   all equally suitable)

2 rounds of buttered toast

METHOD

1   Turn out undiluted soup into a saucepan.
2   Add eggs and beat vigorously into the soup with a fork.
3   Stir continuously with a spoon over moderate heat until the eggs absorb the soup and become a thick, well-flavoured scrambled egg.
4   Serve at once on rounds of buttered toast.

Spaghetti Bolognese

Serves 2

Cooking time: 20 minutes

INGREDIENTS

1 can of minced beef
  ($7\frac{1}{2}$ oz.)
2 tablespoons minestrone
  soup mix

quarter of a pint of water
3 oz. spaghetti

METHOD

1 Place the minced beef in a saucepan and stir in the dry soup powder and add the water.
2 Bring to the boil and allow to simmer for 20 minutes.
3 Meanwhile, in a medium-size saucepan, bring some salted water to the boil, add the spaghetti, keep the lid off and boil fast until the spaghetti is just soft, about 10 minutes. Drain.
4 Serve the meat sauce poured over the spaghetti.

Note. Serve the meat sprinkled with Parmesan cheese if you have some.

Steamed Chocolate Pudding

Serves 4 (or two servings one day, re-steamed for another 2 servings next day)

You will need a medium-sized pudding basin and a saucepan – larger and taller than the basin – with a tightly fitting lid.

Cooking time: 1 hour, 30 minutes–2 hours

INGREDIENTS

3 oz. self-raising flour
1 level teaspoon baking powder
2 level tablespoons cocoa
2 level tablespoons Marvel or similar dried milk

3 oz. soft brown sugar
4 oz. soft, easy-creaming margarine
2 eggs

custard (optional)

METHOD

1 Sieve together the flour, baking powder and cocoa.
2 Add the rest of the ingredients and cream thoroughly until the mixture is well blended.
3 Turn into the greased pudding basin allowing room for the pudding to rise and cover tightly with kitchen foil.
4 Lift into the saucepan and surround with boiling water, coming half to two thirds up the outside of the basin. To avoid black staining on an aluminium pan through the boiling of the water, add a tablespoon of vinegar to the boiling water; this keeps the pan silvery.
5 Keep simmering for 1 hour, 30 minutes–2 hours, with the lid tightly on the pan. If too much water evaporates, add a little more boiling water.

6   Remove foil and either turn the pudding out on to a
    plate, or serve straight from the basin. Good served
    with custard.

To re-steam, replace in the basin, re-cover with foil
and steam for about half an hour.

Baked Chocolate Cake

1   Use exactly the same ingredients as for Steamed
    Chocolate Pudding.
2   Mix by the same method, but instead of turning it
    into a pudding basin, put it into a well-greased 1-lb.
    loaf tin or 6-inch round cake tin or a one-and-a-half-
    pint pie dish. Hollow the centre slightly.
3   Bake the cake at 325°F, gas mark 3 for about 50
    minutes.

To remove the cake from a loose-bottomed tin stand the
tin on a jar and push down the sides.

Cherry and Walnut Cake Topping

one and a half oz. glacé   1 heaped tablespoon apricot
   cherries, halved   jam
1 oz. walnuts, halved

METHOD

Put the cherries, walnuts and jam into a saucepan. Heat
until boiling, then spread over the top of the cake. Leave
until cold.

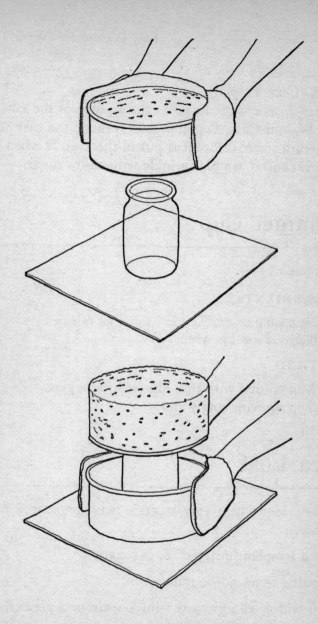

Simple Cake Topping
If you do not want to go to the trouble of the Cherry
and Walnut Cake Topping *either* sprinkle the cake with
demerara sugar before it is put in the oven *or* when the
cake is cooked, simply sprinkle with castor sugar.

Summer Cup

Serves 1

INGREDIENTS

1 tablespoon lime cordial   water for mixing
1 tablespoon rose-hip syrup

METHOD

1   Mix cordial with rose-hip syrup in a glass.
2   Top up with cold water.

Tea Loaf

Time: Made in 2 easy stages – with at least 6 hours
between

Oven temperature: 350° F, gas mark 4

Cooking time: 50–60 minutes

You will need a greased 1-lb. loaf tin or a greased one-
and-a-half-pint pie dish.

INGREDIENTS

Stage 1

2 teaspoons tea
a quarter of a pint of boiling
water
4 oz. mixed, dried, cake
fruit
3 oz. castor sugar

Stage 2

1 egg, beaten
8 oz. self-raising flour, sieved
2 heaped tablespoons Marvel,
or similar skimmed milk
powder
1 level tablespoon marmalade

METHOD

Stage 1

1   Make the tea with the boiling water in a teapot or
jug. Leave to infuse for 5 minutes. Left-over tea may
be used instead.

2   Place the fruit and sugar in a bowl and strain the
tea over it. Leave to stand for at least 6 hours, but
preferably overnight.

Stage 2

3   To the fruit mixture add the egg, flour, Marvel and
the marmalade and mix well.

4   Turn the mixture into the prepared tin, hollow out
the centre slightly, and bake in a moderate oven
350°F, gas mark 4 for about 50–60 minutes. Insert a
skewer to make certain it is fully baked. (The skewer
should come out clean without wet mixture sticking
to it.)

5   Serve the tea loaf sliced thinly and spread with
butter.

Chapter 6
Some Useful Hints and Information

WEIGHING AND MEASURING

Many of the recipes in this book do not need meticulously accurate weighing. If you have kitchen scales, obviously it is better to use them and for this reason we have specified ounces. Without scales use the Tala Cook's Measure recommended on page 197 or turn to the Handy Measures below. Or – more likely – continue to make your own experienced judgement, you will not go far wrong.

Handy Measures

breadcrumbs, fresh 1 oz. = 7 level tablespoons approximately
        ,,   dried 1 oz. = 6 ,,   ,,   ,,
packet crumbs   1 oz. = 4 ,,   ,,   ,,
cheese, Cheddar,
  grated   1 oz. = 3 ,,   ,,   ,,
cocoa powder   1 oz. = 3 ,,   ,,   ,,
cornflour, custard
  powder   1 oz. = 2 ,,   ,,   ,,
dried fruit (cur-
  rants, sultanas,
  raisins)   1 oz. = 2 ,,   ,,   ,,

flour, unsifted   1 oz. = 3 level tablespoons approximately
rice, uncooked   1 oz. = 2 ,,   ,,   ,,
rolled oats   1 oz. = 4 ,,   ,,   ,,
semolina   1 oz. = 2 ,,   ,,   ,,
suet, packet
   shredded   1 oz. = 3 ,,   ,,   ,,
sugar, granulated,
   castor, demerara 1 oz. = 2 ,,   ,,   ,,
syrup, honey,
   treacle   1 oz. = 1 ,,   ,,   ,,
8 tablespoons liquid = 5 fluid oz. = quarter of a pint

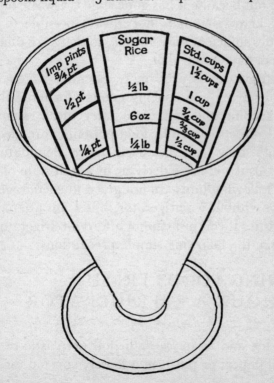

HOW TO KEEP FOODS FRESH

Under the heading of 'Luxury Equipment' on page 201 I have said that a refrigerator is more of a necessity than a luxury. I was thinking particularly of the small refrigerators ideal for a one- or two-person household.

It is a risk to leave, for example, raw or cooked meat or poultry, as well as many other foods, unrefrigerated because food-poisoning organisms can multiply rapidly. Quite apart from food poisoning, food that has to be thrown out because it has gone stale is a waste of money. We all know that it is not always possible to buy in quantities sufficient only for one, so there are times when left-overs have to be kept.

A refrigerator is even more essential if you make a habit of buying and cooking enough for more than one meal, keeping the rest for a later meal. Remember, stomach upsets caused by food poisoning are always unpleasant; they can be even more debilitating and dangerous if you are elderly or in a frail state of health.

The following hints are not given to encourage you to manage without a refrigerator, but I am attempting to be realistic; if you just cannot afford a refrigerator, do at least take the following simple precautions:

KEEPING FOODS FRESH
WITHOUT A REFRIGERATOR
Bacon
● Unpack and wrap *loosely* in foil or plastic or grease-proof paper; or put it in a loosely covered dish. Keep

it as cool as possible. Smoked bacon keeps a little longer than unsmoked or green bacon.

● Vacuum-packed bacon can be left unopened but must be kept cold. Once opened – before the expiry-date stamp – keep as above.

● Mild or sweetcure bacon must be kept in a refrigerator.

Bread

● A wrapped sliced loaf: open one end of wrapping to let air in.

● An unwrapped loaf: put into a clean plastic bag, the ends just folded over loosely.

● Clean out crumbs regularly because they soon spread mould. If you use a plastic bag, it is not essential to have a bread bin. But if you have a bread bin it is a good idea to rinse it with a clean, damp cloth sprinkled with a few drops of vinegar; then dry thoroughly. This helps to prevent the spread of mould.

● Loaves which keep freshest longest are those enriched with fat, gluten breads, starch-reduced loaves, granary bread and malt bread.

Butter, margarine and cooking fat

● In hot weather use an earthenware butter crock. Or stand wrapped packet upright in a basin containing a little cold water. Put it in an airy place and drape wet butter muslin or a thin wet cloth over the top, touching the packet and dipping into the water (see explanation under 'Milk').

Eggs

- Avoid buying eggs from shops where they are displayed in a sunny window. At home avoid warm, sunny storage.
- Keep eggs as cool as possible in a covered egg rack or in a container with a lid in which eggs are bought.
- Do not keep eggs near strong-smelling foods.
- Store eggs pointed end down so that when the yolk rises the airspace at the top stops it from touching the shell.

Fish

- Unwrap fish as soon as you get it home and store it, in the cool, in a loosely covered dish.
- Cook fish on the day of purchase. Even smoked fish does not keep well – only a little longer than unsmoked fish.

Gravy

- It is advisable not to keep gravy from one day to the next without a refrigerator.
- If you make a casserole, which is enough for two days, the gravy in it must be cooled rapidly in the casserole. Next day the casserole must be re-boiled thoroughly right through to the centre.

Meat and Poultry

- Keep raw meat and poultry in the cold, not touching anything cooked, including cooked meat. This is because if germs from the raw meat are transferred by contact – or by your hands – to already cooked foods they may rapidly multiply, if left in a warm place or unrefrigerated in the kitchen.

- Unwrap meats straight away and keep in a loosely covered dish or use a flyproof dish cover.
- Cook *completely* and *thoroughly* as soon as possible. Never partly cook meat or poultry to finish cooking later.
- Always wash hands, boards and implements after touching raw meat or poultry. This is essential to avoid the spread of food-poisoning bacteria.

Milk

- Never leave milk in the sun and light; if you cannot take it in immediately, ask the milkman to place it in the shade.
- Keep milk in an airy place. Keep the untorn bottle cap on to protect it from dust and flies.

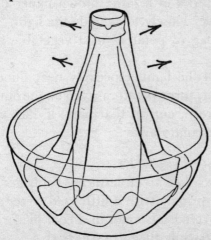

- In very hot weather use a milk cooler or put a little cold water in a basin, stand the milk bottle or carton in it and cover with wet butter muslin or a thin wet cloth dipping into the water. The evaporation from the cloth will keep the milk cool. From time to time replace the cold water in the basin. You must make sure that the muslin or cloth is kept wet.
- Never use milk which smells 'off'.

Pet foods

- Raw or uncanned pet meat may contain food-poisoning organisms, so keep this food separate from family foods and use different utensils and surfaces for their preparation. Wash and dry pets dishes and utensils separately from your own.

Potatoes

- Keep potatoes in a large brown paper bag and fold the top over loosely to exclude the light.
- Put the bag of potatoes in a vegetable rack or cool corner.
- Storage in the light, especially near fluorescent light or sunlight, turns potatoes green on the outside. If only slightly green, cut off that part; if dark green, throw the whole potato away.

Salads and green vegetables

- In hot weather treat lettuces, cabbages and greens like this: sprinkle with a little cold water and put in a tightly covered saucepan in a cool place. Use as soon as possible while they are still fresh.

Left-overs

● If you have a refrigator, never cool hot food in it because you will merely raise the temperature of the refrigator.

Canned Foods

● Once a can is opened, the contents should be kept only as long as fresh foods. If you are not using the whole of the can, do not turn it all out; just remove what you want and leave the rest in the can, covered with a saucer or with kitchen foil. Put it in a cool place and finish the rest next day. The only exceptions are fruit and fruit juices, which are best turned out of the can, because they alter slightly in flavour once the can is opened.

● It is best not to keep an opened can of a meat product overnight without a refrigerator.

Dairy Foods

● It is unwise to keep cream cakes, trifles, milk puddings and similar desserts from one day to the next, if you do not have very cold storage conditions. If you keep them in the cold, remember to keep them covered.

Meat or Poultry

● Avoid long, slow cooling. Put the warm meat or poultry in a covered dish and run the cold tap on it. If possible, for instance with casseroles, meat cakes etc., stir the contents of the dish from time to time to encourage quick cooling. After this rapid drop in temperature store it covered (e.g. with a lid or under a flyproof dish cover) in as cool a place as possible.

GIFTS TO GIVE TO YOURSELF OR TO OTHERS

The lists below are not intended to be a complete selection of kitchen equipment. We merely hope it will solve some present-giving problems and that its ideas will prevent the sometimes desperate selection of socks and sweets and shawls.

Prices range from a few shillings to many pounds, but we cannot quote prices because they are so likely to change. We have instead divided the gifts into three groups: gadgets (inexpensive), equipment (some quite inexpensive) and luxury equipment.

If you want more ideas – particularly if you are buying for the disabled – send for the booklet 'List of Kitchen Equipment' published by the Disabled Living Foundation, 346 Kensington High Street, London, W.14, price 29p including postage. Their booklet includes several of the items in our lists below, together with details of where to buy the equipment.

For left-handed equipment, write to Anything Left Handed Ltd, 65 Beak Street, London, w.1. and ask for their catalogue price $7\frac{1}{2}$p, including postage.

We acknowledge help – including equipment sent for trial – from firms producing the following kitchen ware: Ekcoware, Moulinex, Prestige, Pyrosil, Skyline, Tala.

Gadgets

Bakewell parchment – a non-stick parchment which needs no greasing – for lining tins for baking biscuits, cakes, etc.

Bottle-top opener – a rubber cap fitting over a bottle top provides additional friction for unscrewing. A do-it-yourself alternative: wear a plastic or rubber washing-up glove to give a grip when unscrewing bottles. Also available: a milk-bottle opener.

Can openers.

Cloths – use a cellulose sponge cloth which can be boiled and is easily kept clean. Extra use: when dampened and placed under bowl or dish, helps to stabilize whilst mixing, cutting or serving food.

Double suction rubber bowl for stabilizing mixing bowl. One surface adheres firmly to smooth work top when dampened, whilst the top will hold a bowl firmly. Also useful for the one-handed to dry up crockery. Inexpensive.

Egg separator by Prestige which effectively separates whites from yolks – see illustrations overleaf.

Egg slicer.

Funnels, in easily cleaned plastic.

Kitchen foil.

Kitchen tongs, cook's spoon and cook's fork.

Left-handed gadgets for handicapped, as well as for left-handers, e.g. can opener, potato-peeler/kitchen knife, saucepan strainer, spatulas, stirrers and whisks.

Lemon squeezer.

Lid unscrewer (Unduit), an inexpensive V-shaped device for unscrewing lids; should be fixed to under-surface of shelf or worktop.

Milk saver (Solidex) – circle of toughened glass which, when placed in saucepan, prevents milk from boiling

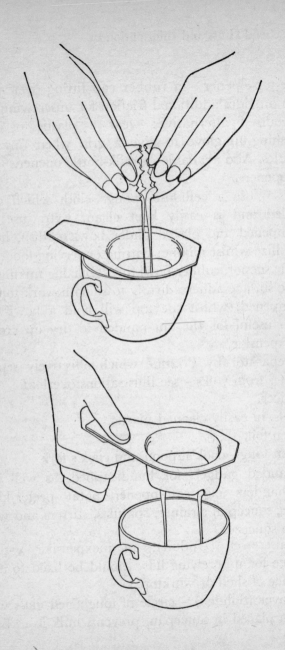

over. It gives audible warning when milk nears boiling point.

Oven gloves. A length of material padded on palm surface and folded over at each end to form gloves. The connecting material between the 'gloves' lessens danger of burning arms above the wrist.

Pan stands.

Potato peeler.

Scissors for kitchen use.

Spatula, flexible.

Spike board for spreading or slicing – in rigid plastic with four suction feet. Useful for the cook able to use only one hand; stabilizes meat, bread, etc. The spikes are not sharp. Inexpensive.

Standard measuring spoons.

Tala Cook's Measure – aluminium conical shape with many measurements for different foods clearly marked. An inexpensive alternative to kitchen scales. See illustration, page 187.

Teaspoon tea infuser. (Labour saving for making tea for one person.) See illustration overleaf.

Timer – set the clock alarm to ring as a reminder.

Whisks: Skyline balloon whisk, see illustration, page 143. Skyline spring whisk which can be used by either hand or by both hands together, see illustration, page 90.

Equipment

Colander with long, plastic, heat-resistant handle.

Gas lighter – a safer method of lighting burners than matches or taper.

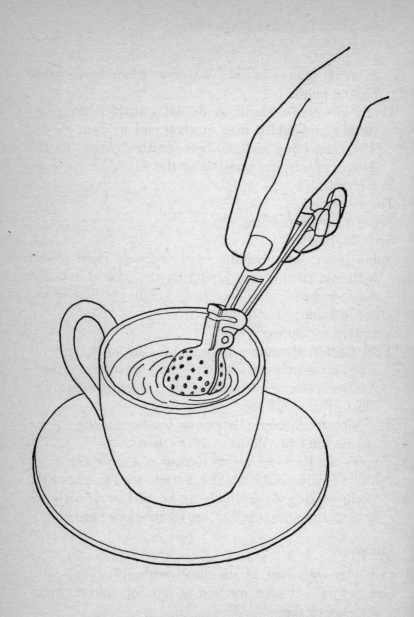

Grater – box-shaped for easy holding.

Measuring jug, graduated, one-and-a-half pints capacity. Rigid plastic, open-end handle, can facilitate gripping for those with hand impairments.

Mouli kitchen ware for sieving, shredding, mincing, grating, chopping and slicing. See illustrations.

Non-stick cake and patty tins. Contents can be easily tipped out; and these tins are kept clean by wiping with a cloth or kitchen paper. Also non-stick saucepan and frying-pan. When used according to instructions these are extremely easy to keep clean.

Oven-to-table ware: Pyrex or other *ovenproof* casseroles, soufflé dish, pie plate and other dishes of small enough size for one or two servings.

Pyrosil or other *flameproof* small pans or dishes for one or two servings, e.g. Pyrosil Handipans.

Plastic containers with tightly fitting lids: basins, jugs, food canisters, beakers and storage boxes in various shapes, sizes and colours.

Plate warmer with night-light refills. Inexpensive, could be helpful to those who eat slowly.

Pressure cooker, e.g. Skyline Minor, for speedy, economical and nourishing cooking.

Saucepans, including small 2-pint size with well-fitting lid. Can be found with twin handles for easy lifting.

Space savers – plastic covered wire trays for stacking china in a small space. Also space-saving baskets, drawers and shelves.

Spong suction-based mincer to stand firmly without screws or clamps on any non-porous surface such as enamel or laminated plastic. It also has a luxury gift set which includes a shredder and grater.

Steamer basket which fits into saucepan to enable pudding basins, vegetables, etc. to be lifted out without scalding hands.

Luxury equipment

Automatic tea-maker.

Dish washer – a wonderful family Golden Wedding present.

Electric beater, hand held.

Electric food mixer with attachments.

Liquidizer either bought separately or as an attachment.

Electric kettle, with safety cut-out mechanism.

Refrigerator (although it could be argued that this is more of a necessity than a luxury).

Small tea-trolley, especially useful if larder, store-cupboard and table are at a distance.

List of Illustrations

'Afternoon nap' tea 12
Cheese and ketchup toasted sandwich 13
Lazy soup 24
Cheese grater 59
Fruity pan pudding 73
One-pot kedgeree 89
Skyline spring whisk, used by one or two hands 90
Cooking tongs 93
Quick cabbage 97
Steamed roasting chicken 109
Egg and lemon sauce 111
Chops in foil 128
Mouli sieve for soups 142
Balloon whisk for sauce 143
Pineapple upside-down pudding 151
Speedy mix chocolate cake 160
Skyline beater 169
Raspberry honeycomb 176
Removing cake from loose-bottomed tin 183
Tala Cook's Measure 187
Cooling milk 191
Egg separator 196
Teaspoon tea infuser 198
Pyrosil Handipans 199, 200

Index

Index

'Afternoon nap' tea, 11
Anaemia, nutritional, 5
Apple
  Apple with amber sauce, 41
  Apple crumble, 118
  Apple (farmer's wife), 43
  Apple parcel, 119
  Apple Welsh rarebit, 117
  Pork and apple slices, 94

Bacon
  To keep fresh without a
    refrigerator, 188
  Bacon with mustard sauce,
    44
  Bacon pudding, 46
  Bacon Welsh rarebit, 117
  Egg and bacon saucer pie,
    154
  Glazed bacon joint, 45
  Golden cutlet and bacon, 74
  Liver and bacon bake, 80
Baked brisket, 47
Baked chocolate cake, 182

Baked cod, 48
Baked custard, 166
Baked potatoes in their jackets,
  49
Bakewell tart, 120
Beef
  Baked brisket, 47
  Beef loaf, 50
  Corned beefburgers, 17
  Cottage pie, 66
  Goulash, 171
  Meat balls, 82
  Oat corned beefburgers,
    174
  Spaghetti Bolognese, 180
  Steak and kidney crumble,
    105
  Steak pan pudding, 106
Beverages
  'Afternoon nap' tea, 11
  Beverages for the store
    cupboard, 165
  Egg flip, 17
  Lemonade, 25

Beverages – *contd.*
  Petail, 29
  Savoury milk, 32
  Summer cup, 184
  Tea grog, 36
Biscuits
  Button biscuits, 124
  Easter biscuits, 132
  Ena's Austrian biscuits, 69
Blackcurrant pudding, 51
Body-building foods 3–5;
    recipes for, 4–5
Bone-building foods 7; recipes
    for, 8
Braised celery, 55
Braised leeks, 55
Bread and butter pudding,
    rhubarb, 99
Bread and butter pudding,
    savoury (cheese and
    Marmite), 58
Breads
  To keep bread fresh, 189
  Brown bread, quick method
    122
  Date and sultana bread,
    131
  Tea loaf, 184
  Breakfast, nourishing, 27
  Brisket of beef, baked, 47
  Brown bread, quick method,
    122
  Brussels sprouts, to cook, 19
  Buck rarebit, 117

Butter, to keep fresh without
    refrigerator, 189
Button biscuits, 124

Cabbage
  To cook cabbage, 19
  Quick cabbage, 96
Cakes: and toppings for cakes:
  Baked chocolate cake, 182
  Cherry and walnut cake
    topping, 182
  Crumble shortbread, 130
  Lemon cake, 78
  Simple cake topping, 184
  Speedy mix chocolate cake,
    159
  Victoria sandwich cake, 162
Calcium, foods which provide, 7
California salad, 125
Canned foods, to keep fresh
    once opened, 193
Carrot
  Carrots cooked in butter, 52
  Carrots and leeks, 54
Casseroles and stews:
  Chicken casserole, 62
  Lancashire hot-pot, 76
  Meat stew, Norwegian style,
    84
Cauliflower, to cook, 19
Celery
  Braised celery, 55
Cereals:
  Cereals for store cupboard,
    165

Cereals – *contd*
  Health food cereal, 20
  Muesli with fruit, 137
Cheese
  Cheese and cress omelette,
    56
  Cheese crumb chicken, 57
  Cheese and ham toasted
    sandwich, 13
  Cheese and ketchup toasted
    sandwich, 13
  Cheese and Marmite bread
    and butter pudding, 58
  Cheese 'Pizza', 14
  Cheese and rice layer pie,
    60
  Cheese savoury, 126
  Cheese scones, 158
  Cheese soufflé, one-stage, 61
  Potato and cheese savoury
    custard, 152
  Toasted cheese, 37
  Welsh rarebit, 116
  Welsh rarebit de luxe, 117
Cherry and walnut cake
    topping, 182
Cherub dumplings, 167
Chicken
  Cheese crumb chicken, 57
  Chicken casserole, 62
  Chicken Welsh rarebit, 117
  Fricassée of chicken in one
    pan, 71
  Steamed roasting chicken,
    108

Chocolate
  Baked chocolate cake, 182
  Chocolate fudge bars, 168
  Chocolate icing or filling,
    163
  Chocolate mousse, 169
  Chocolate spread, 35
  Hot chocolate rice, 29
  Speedy mix chocolate cake,
    159
  Steamed chocolate pudding,
    180
Chops in foil, 127
Chops and onions, 63
Cod
  Baked cod, 48
  Cod charlotte, 65
  Grilled cod, 75
Coddled eggs – foolproof
    method, 15–16
Coffee icing or filling, 163
Convalescents, tempting dishes
    for, 4
Corned beefburgers, 17
Corned beefburgers, oat, 174
Cottage pie, 66
Crumble shortbread, 130
Crumble topping, 147
Curry sauce, 67

Dairy foods, to keep fresh
    without refrigerator, 193
Date and sultana bread, 131
Date and sultana gingerbread,
    132

Desserts. *See also* Puddings
   Apple with amber sauce,
     41
   Apple crumble, 118
   Apple (farmer's wife), 43
   Apple parcel, 119
   Baked custard, 166
   Bakewell tart, 120
   Chocolate mousse, 169
   Fresh fruit salad, 135
   Fruit flapjack, 136
   Hot chocolate rice, 29
   Meringue rice, 85
   Mock zabaglione, 26
   Orange rice, 28
   Raspberry honeycomb,
     175
   Sweet saucer pies, 156
   Yogurt jelly, 38
Devilled kidneys, 68

Easter biscuits, 132
Eggs
   To store eggs, 190
   Buck rarebit, 117
   Coddled eggs – foolproof
     method, 15–16
   Cheese and cress omelette,
     56
   Egg and bacon saucer pie,
     154
   Egg flip, 17
   Egg and lemon sauce, 110
   Egg and onion, 18
   Kipper scramble, 21

   Liver-sausage and egg
     spread, 34
   Mumbled eggs, 26
   Poached eggs, cream-style, 31
   Scrambled haddock and eggs,
     22
   Soup scramble, 179
   Tomato soup and egg, 33
   Vegetable omelette, 115
Ena's Austrian biscuits, 69
Energy-providing foods, 8–9
Equipment, 197–201; luxury
    equipment, 201

Fats for store cupboard, 165;
    to keep fresh without
    refrigerator, 189
Fillings, one-stage, 163
Fish. *See also* Cod, Haddock
    etc.
   To keep fresh without a
    refrigerator, 190
   Canned fish rich in Vitamin
    D, 8
   Canned fish for store
    cupboard, 165
   Fish with vegetables, 133
   Fisherman's pudding, 70
   Golden cutlet and bacon,
    74
   Golden cutlet and egg sauce,
    138
   Grilled cod, 75
   Quick fish soufflé, 98
   Summer fish, 112

Flavourings for store cupboard, 165

Foods, to keep fresh without refrigerator, 188–93

Fricassée of chicken in one pan, 71

Fricassée of liver, 143

Fruit. *See also* Apple, Blackcurrant etc.
  Canned fruits for store cupboard, 165
  Fresh fruit salad, 135
  Fruit flapjack, 136
  Fruit meringue, 170
  Fruit muesli, 137
  Fruit scones, 158

Fruity pan pudding, 72

Gadgets for the kitchen, 194–7

Gingerbread, date and sultana, 132

Glazed bacon joint, 45

Golden cutlet and bacon, 74

Golden cutlet and egg sauce, 138

Goulash, 171

Grapefruit
  Spiced grapefruit, 104

Gravy, to keep fresh, 190

Greens, to cook, 19

Grilled cod, 75

Grilled herring, 139

Groceries for store cupboard, 166

Haddock
  One-pot kedgeree, 87
  Scrambled haddock and eggs, 22

Ham
  Ham with mustard sauce, 44
  Ham and vegetable rice, 172
  Ham Welsh rarebit, 117

Health food cereal, 20

Herring
  Grilled herring, 139
  Herring roes on toast, 173

Icings, 'one-stage', 163

Iron-providing foods 5; recipes for, 5

Italian chops, 129

Kedgeree, one-pot, 87

Kidney
  Devilled kidneys, 68
  Steak and kidney crumble, 105

Kipper
  To cook kippers without smells, 21
  To keep leftover kipper, 21
  Kipper scramble, 21

Lamb
  Chops and onions, 63
  Italian chops, 129
  Lancashire hot-pot, 76
  Sweet and sour spare-ribs of lamb, 161

Lancashire hot-pot, 76
Lazy soup, 23
Leeks
  Braised leeks, 55
  Leeks with carrots, 54
Left-handed gadgets,
      equipment, 194, 195
Left-overs, to store, 193
Lemon
  Egg and lemon sauce, 110
  Lemon cake, 78
  Lemon curd spread, 36
  Lemon icing or filling, 163
  Lemon pudding, 79
  Lemon sponge pudding,
      140
  Lemonade, 25
Lentil cream soup, 141
Liver
  Liver and bacon bake, 80
  Liver fricassée, 143
  Liver-sausage and egg
      spread, 34

Macaroni, Italian style, 81
Margarine, to keep fresh
      without refrigerator, 189
Meat. See also Beef, Lamb etc.
  To keep raw meat fresh
      without refrigerator, 190
  To store cooked meats
      without refrigerator, 193
  Canned meat for store
      cupboard, 166
  Chops in foil, 127

Easy-to-chew meat dishes, 4
Inexpensive meat dishes, 4
Meat balls, 82
Meat roly-poly, 173
Meat stew, Norwegian style,
      84
Meats rich in iron, 5
  Pilaff, 91
  Risotto, 103
Meringue rice, 85
Milk
  To keep milk fresh without
      refrigerator, 191
  Milk pastry, 145
  Potato and milk soup, 153
  Savoury milk, 32
Muesli with fruit, 137
Mumbled eggs, 26
Mushroom soup, 86
Mustard sauce with bacon or
      ham, 44

Nourishing breakfast, 27

Oat corned beefburgers, 174
Omelette
  Cheese and cress omelette,
      56
  Vegetable omelette, 115
One-pot kedgeree, 87
One-stage icing or filling, 163
Onion
  Chops and onions, 63
  Egg and onion, 18
  Tripe and onions, 114

Orange
  Orange cabinet-pudding, 90
  Orange icing or filling, 163
  Orange rice, 28
  Peptail, 29

Parsnip
  Parsnip and potato, 55
  Parsnips with baked brisket, 47
  Parsnips cooked in butter, 52
Pastry
  Milk pastry, 145
  Rules for pastry-making, 144
  Short crusty pastry mix, 146
Peppermint creams, 147
Peptail, 29
Pet foods, to keep fresh without refrigerator, 192
Pies
  Cheese and rice layer pie, 60
  Cottage pie, 66
  Saucer pies, 154–6
Pilaff, 91
Pineapple
  Pineapple meringue pudding, 148
  Pineapple salad, 30
  Pineapple upside-down pudding, 149
Plain scones, 156
Poached eggs, cream-style, 31
Poached sausages, 92
Pork and apple slices, 94

Potato
  To store potatoes, 192
  Baked potatoes in their jackets, 49
  Potato and cheese savoury custard, 152
  Potato and milk soup, 153
  Potato and parsnip, 55
  Potato scones, 95
  Potato and swede, 55
Poultry. *See also* Chicken
  To keep raw poultry fresh without refrigerator, 190
  To store cooked poultry without refrigerator, 193
Puddings. *See also* Desserts
  Blackcurrant pudding, 51
  Cherub dumplings, 167
  Fruit meringue, 170
  Fruity pan pudding, 72
  Lemon pudding, 79
  Lemon sponge pudding, 140
  Orange cabinet pudding, 90
  Pineapple meringue pudding, 148
  Pineapple upside-down pudding, 149
  Rhubarb bread and butter pudding, 99
  Rice pudding, 100
  Soufflé ground rice, 178
  Steamed chocolate pudding, 180

Puddings, savoury
  Bacon pudding, 46
  Cheese and Marmite bread
    and butter pudding, 58
  Fisherman's pudding, 70
  Steak pan pudding, 106

Quick and easy dishes, 4
Quick cabbage, 96
Quick fish soufflé, 98

Raspberry honeycomb, 175
Rhubarb bread and butter
    pudding, 99
Rice
  Cheese and rice layer pie,
    60
  Ham and vegetable rice,
    172
  Hot chocolate rice, 29
  Meringue rice, 85
  Orange rice, 28
  Pilaff, 91
  Rice pudding, 100
  Risotto, 102
  Soufflé ground rice, 178
Risotto, 102
Roes, herring, on toast, 173

Salads
  To keep fresh without
    refrigerator, 192
  California salad, 125
  Fresh fruit salad, 135
  Pineapple salad, 30

Sandwiches
  Cheese and ham toasted
    sandwich, 13
  Cheese and ketchup toasted
    sandwich, 13
Sardine
  Digestible sardine spread,
    34
Saucer pies, 154–6
Sauces
  Curry sauce, 67
  Egg and lemon sauce, 110
  Mustard sauce for bacon or
    ham, 44
  Tomato sauce, 114
Sausages
  Poached sausages, 92
Savoury frits, 104
Savoury milk, 32
Savoury soufflé, 176
Scones
  Cheese scones, 158
  Fruit scones, 158
  Plain scones, 156
  Potato scones, 95
Scrambled haddock and eggs,
    22
Short crust pastry mix, 146
Shortbread, 130
Soufflés
  Cheese soufflé, one-stage,
    61
  Quick fish soufflé, 98
  Savoury soufflé, 176
  Soufflé ground rice, 178

Soups
  Lazy soup, 23
  Lentil cream soup, 141
  Mushroom soup, 86
  Potato and milk soup, 153
  Soup scramble, 179
  Soup supper, 32
  Tomato soup and egg, 33
Spaghetti Bolognese, 180
Spiced grapefruit, 104
Spreads
  Chocolate spread, 35
  Digestible sardine, 34
  Lemon curd spread, 36
  Liver-sausage and egg
    spread, 34
  Tuna and tomato spread, 35
Steak and kidney crumble, 105
Steak pan pudding, 106
Steamed chocolate pudding,
  180
Steamed roasting chicken, 108
Stews. See Casseroles and stews
Summer cup, 184
Summer fish, 112
Swede and potato, 55
Sweet and sour spare-ribs of
    lamb, 161
Sweets
  Peppermint creams, 147

Tart
  Bakewell tart, 120
Tea grog, 36
Tea loaf, 184

Tea made in vacuum flask,
  11
Toasted cheese, 37
Toasted sandwiches, 13
Tomato
  Tomato sauce, 114
  Tomato soup and egg, 33
  Tomato Welsh rarebit, 117
  Tomatoes – quick change,
    113
  Tuna and tomato spread, 35
Toppings for cakes, 182, 184
Tripe and onions, 114
Tuna and tomato spread, 35

Upside-down pudding,
  pineapple, 149

Vegetables. See also Cabbage,
    Carrot etc.
  To cook green vegetables, 19
  To keep green vegetables
    fresh without refrigerator,
    192
  Canned and dried vegetables
    for store cupboard, 165
  Cooking two vegetables
    together, 54
  Fish with vegetables, 133
  Ham and vegetable rice,
    172
  Vegetable omelette, 115
Victoria sandwich cake, 162
Vitamin B providing foods,
  8–9

Vitamin C providing foods and
     drinks, 6–7
Vitamin D providing foods,
     7–8

Weighing and measuring,
     186–7

Welsh rarebit, 116
Welsh rarebit de luxe, 117

Yogurt, 38
Yogurt jelly, 38

Zabaglione, mock, 26

More about Penguins and Pelicans

Penguinews, which appears every month, contains details of all the new books issued by Penguins as they are published. From time to time it is supplemented by *Penguins in Print*, which is a complete list of all available books published by Penguins. (There are well over three thousand of these.)

A specimen copy of *Penguinews* will be sent to you free on request, and you can become a subscriber for the price of the postage. For a year's issues (including the complete lists) please send 30p if you live in the United Kingdom, or 60p if you live elsewhere. Just write to Dept EP, Penguin Books Ltd, Harmondsworth, Middlesex, enclosing a cheque or postal order, and your name will be added to the mailing list.

Note: *Penguinews* and *Penguins in Print* are not available in the U.S.A. or Canada

The Penguin Cookery Book

Bee Nilson

'My choice for a young housewife's first cook book –
particularly if she is tied to a strict budget – is *The
Penguin Cookery Book* by Bee Nilson' – Ambrose Heath
in *Ideal Home*

'A book which is likely to find a grateful and useful
place in many homes . . . Here are over 850 basic
recipes, given in both weights and measures, indexed
and cross-referenced . . . Should the beginner require
more than that, he or she will also find advice on
kitchen equipment, food values, how much food to buy
for how many, cooking time, temperatures, and a
glossary of French terms. Finally there are diagrams, to
assist in identifying the different cuts of meat and in
preparing fish' – *Listener*

The third edition includes over 990 recipes.

Another Penguin Handbook by Bee Nilson

Cooking for Special Diets

This is the first book written entirely with the problems of a special diet in mind. The sections begin with short explanations of such diseases as diabetes, anaemia, ulcers, heart diseases, and obesity, followed by the reasons for prescribing fat-free, low protein, liquid, or other restricted diet and a description of the diet itself. A general meal pattern, suggestions for eating out, ideas for packed lunches, and a set of fourteen dinner and fourteen lunch or supper menus round off the discussion of each variety of disease and diet. The recipes for these menus are given in the second half of the book, together with the names and addresses of manufacturers of special products.

Cooking for Special Diets will be of direct interest to the families of patients released from hospital, in cases where the housewife is expected to turn a prescribed diet into palatable meals. All the recipes given here by Bee Nilson have been tested by herself as well as by student dieticians in college.

Modern Vegetarian Cookery

Walter and Jenny Fliess

As founders and owners of the famous vegetarian 'Vega' restaurants in Cologne and London, Walter and Jenny Fliess built up an international reputation for themselves many years ago.

In this cookbook they compressed a good slice of their life's work into some 500 recipes for vegetarian dishes of all kinds, soups, sauces, sweets, and uncooked meals. They are not directly concerned here with the broader theory of vegetarianism or food reform, and their book will simply and engagingly recommend itself to most readers as a very practical one.

These fresh and imaginative recipes open up new culinary worlds and remove the sting from the injunction to 'eat plenty of fruit and vegetables'.

'Recipes to tempt even meat-eaters' – *Financial Times*

'500 recipes explain how to make everyday vegetables delicious and exciting' – *Vogue*

'The clearly set out recipes are easy to follow . . . One could well live on vegetable fare' – *Tatler*

'A solid work of professional competence which many of our chefs might find intriguing' – *Culinarian* (U.S.A.)

'The idea that vegetarian cooking is necessarily dull is routed by the contents of this attractive book' – *House and Home* (South Africa)

Cooking in a Bedsitter

Katherine Whitehorn

Katherine Whitehorn, the well-known *Observer* writer, has experienced 'that sinking feeling that goes with living in a bedsitter . . . that all these baked beans, etc., can't really be *healthy*'. This handbook, first published as *Kitchen in the Corner*, is designed to counteract a feeling that so many have shared with her.

Armed with her light-hearted but practical guide, which contains about 300 recipes on the right scale, gas-ring cooks and chefs can enter on a new lease of gastronomic life. The whole range of cookery without a kitchen (from first course to such exotica as Ratatouille, Lancashire Hot-Pot and Shrimp Wiggle) is competently covered by a cook who can perceive all the possibilities amid all the limitations. Equipment, stores, frying times, and even catering for parties are among the comprehensive subjects the author handles in a manner witty enough to make a landlady laugh.

'Miss Whitehorn's recipes ring a remarkable number of changes on one-pan dishes' – *Guardian*

'All parents with bedsitter children should send them a copy' – *Observer*

Not for sale in the U.S.A.

Elizabeth David

Elizabeth David is well known for the infectious
enthusiasm with which she presents her recipes.

'She has the happy knack of giving just as much
detail as the average cook finds desirable; she presumes
neither on our knowledge nor on our ignorance' –
Elizabeth Nicholas in the *Sunday Times*

Mediterranean Food
A practical collection of recipes made by the author
when she lived in France, Italy, the Greek Islands and
Egypt, evoking all the colour of the Mediterranean but
making use of ingredients obtainable in England.

French Country Cooking
Some of the splendid regional variations in French
cookery are described in this book.

French Provincial Cooking
'It is difficult to think of any home that can do without
Elizabeth David's *French Provincial Cooking* . . . One
could cook for a lifetime on the book alone' – *Observer*

Elizabeth David

Italian Food

Exploding once and for all the myth that Italians live entirely on minestrone, spaghetti and veal escalopes, this exciting book demonstrates the enormous and colourful variety of Italy's regional cooking.

Summer Cooking

A selection of summer dishes that are light (not necessarily cold), easy to prepare and based on the food in season.

English Cooking Ancient and Modern 1
Spices, Salt and Aromatics in the English Kitchen

Elizabeth David presents English recipes which are notable for their employment of spices, salt and aromatics. As usual, she seasons instruction with information, explaining the origins and uses of her ingredients.

The Pauper's Cookbook

Jocasta Innes

Jocasta Innes dreamed of a cookery book planned for church mice. 'What greedy paupers needed above all, I felt, was a book where all the recipes were nice enough to be tempting, but so cheap they would be painlessly trained to economize.' But no other indigent expert came forward to write it: so she has written it herself.

In *The Pauper's Cookbook* she has assembled a wealth (or should it be a poverty?) of recipes for meals costing between ten and twenty pence per head. Her collection of international, racially mixed and classless dishes promises good home cooking at 'Joe's Café' prices.

Some of the worst cooks waste hours on research: but *The Pauper's Cookbook* bypasses all that. You simply assess the 'cooking situation' and turn up the recommended treatment. The ffortescue-Smyths – or your parents – might call for Fancy Work; young Tomlinson and his dolly-bird, Fast Work; but the Joneses and all those children of theirs come in for Standards and Padding, including reconditioned leftovers. Thrifty tips on Programmed Eating (a week's meals at one session), on not eating (or dieting), and on Private Enterprise (or make-it-yourself) help to cut the costs; and Jocasta Innes starts right where the trouble begins – in the shops.

So leave it to the affluent to court indigestion at the Waldorf-Ritz: here's how to live it up in your own squalid tenement without recourse to poaching, rustling, guddling, scrumping or shop-lifting.